Contents

KT-117-371

Introduction   5

Location maps   10

Cathedrals   18

Cathedrals of other Christian denominations   218

Image credits   223

Foreword

Collins Little Book of English Cathedrals is a guide to England's sixty-two Church of England and Roman Catholic cathedrals. It includes the major sites of world famous St Paul's Cathedral and Canterbury Cathedral, home to the leader of the Church of England. Historical background and architectural details for each of the cathedrals is included, accompanied by beautiful colour photographs. Also included is a brief introduction to the English Cathedrals which belong to other Christian denominations.

Introduction

We tend to associate the rise of Christianity in Britain with St Augustine's mission of AD 597, despite an earlier arrival in the 1st century AD via the Roman artisans and traders who came to Britain spreading the story of Jesus.

The word 'cathedral' comes from the Latin word *cathedra* meaning 'seat' or 'chair' and refers to the location of a Christian bishop or archbishop's throne or seat of office. It is the most important church at the heart of the diocese, which is a geographical district of the Christian Church that falls under the pastoral and administrative care of a bishop and is made up of a number of smaller parishes.

A cathedral is not to be confused with a *minster*, which is the term often used today to refer more generally to any large or important church. A minster is actually a church established during Anglo-Saxon times and attached to a monastery (or *monasterium*) as a teaching or missionary church. Famous minsters include Southwell Minster, Westminster in London, and York Minster. Slightly confusingly, York Minster is also a cathedral which shows that it is possible to be both a cathedral, and a minster but that the title is not interchangeable. York *Minster* was built to baptise Edwin, King of Northumbria in AD 627 and later housed a school and library. The Minster was raised to *Cathedral* status to house the seat of the first Archbishop of York, Thomas of Bayeux, in 1070.

There are many significant places of worship across the British Isles, a number of which are referred to as 'cathedrals'. However, this book provides a specific guide to the twenty Roman Catholic cathedrals and forty-two Church of England cathedrals that are still houses of Christian worship in England today. We have also included a brief introduction to Cathedrals from other Christian denominations which can be found in England. Specifically, the Antiochian, Coptic, Greek, Russian, Syriac and Ukrainian Autocephalous Orthodox Churches and the Anglican and Liberal denominations of the Catholic Church.

Prior to the 16th-century English Reformation, England was part of the Roman Catholic Church under the authority of the Pope. In 1534, England broke away from the Roman papacy at the behest of King Henry VIII and established an independent Church of England with the English monarch becoming the *Supreme Head of the Church* under the Act of Supremacy. This split with the Church was initially as a result of Pope Clement VII's refusal to annul Henry's marriage to his first wife, Catherine of Aragon. Their marriage had not produced a son and heir for Henry and he had already lined up a prospective new wife, Anne Boleyn.

Initially, few changes were made other than the suppression of the monasteries since Henry anticipated that the English Church would remain Catholic, although a separate entity to Rome. However, after Henry's death, Protestant reforms similar to those taking place across Europe were introduced during the short reign of his young son, Edward VI. Despite an attempt by Henry's Catholic daughter, Queen Mary I, to re-establish Roman Catholicism in England, her persecution of Protestants (earning her the nickname 'Bloody Mary') brought more sympathy for the cause and under the reign of her half-sister Elizabeth I the Protestant Church of England was fully established and Catholic worship outlawed. Catholic priests and members of their clandestine congregations were fined, imprisoned or even put to death and Roman Catholic cathedrals were reappropriated by the Church of England and relics destroyed.

The rumblings of the Reformation and contrasting ideas on the role of the monarch as parliamentary and religious leader continued into the 17th century and resulted in the English Civil War between Parliamentarians and Royalists. Whilst the cathedrals of England have seen damage and destruction as a result of natural disasters such as fire, storm and earthquake, it is the man-made damage during these turbulent periods in history (and those that came later such as the Second World War) that have caused the most destruction. Thankfully, extensive restoration work to English cathedrals since the 19th century has allowed future generations to appreciate their historic splendour.

In the 19th century, the 1829 Roman Catholic Relief Act and the 1850 re-creation of the Roman Catholic diocesan hierarchy in England by Pope Pius IX also took place. This explains why all of the current Roman Catholic cathedrals in England date back to the 19th and 20th centuries. The 19th century also saw a great urbanisation of England following the Industrial Revolution. New cities were created, necessitating new dioceses in both the Catholic and Church of England faiths. A number of cities, such as Birmingham, Liverpool, London, Newcastle and Sheffield, have more than one cathedral because they are covered by both a Roman Catholic diocese and a Church of England diocese. In fact, Birmingham is actually home to three Cathedrals since the Greek Orthodox St Andrews Cathedral is also located there.

Many Church of England cathedrals and communities are referred to as 'Anglican', however this simply refers to the worldwide community of churches of which the Church of England is a member; Anglican is not a separate religion. The Archbishop of Canterbury is often described as the spiritual leader of the worldwide Anglican community but outside of England he has no lawful authority, and the religion and its interpretation varies slightly from country to country.

The cathedrals featured in this book are open to visitors as well as worshippers. However, their inclusion in the book does not imply a right of public access at all times. Opening, closing and site accessibility details vary from cathedral to cathedral. It is always advisable to check with the specific cathedral in advance. Telephone numbers and websites are listed in each cathedral description.

Abbreviations	
COE	CHURCH OF ENGLAND
RC	ROMAN CATHOLIC

Northern England

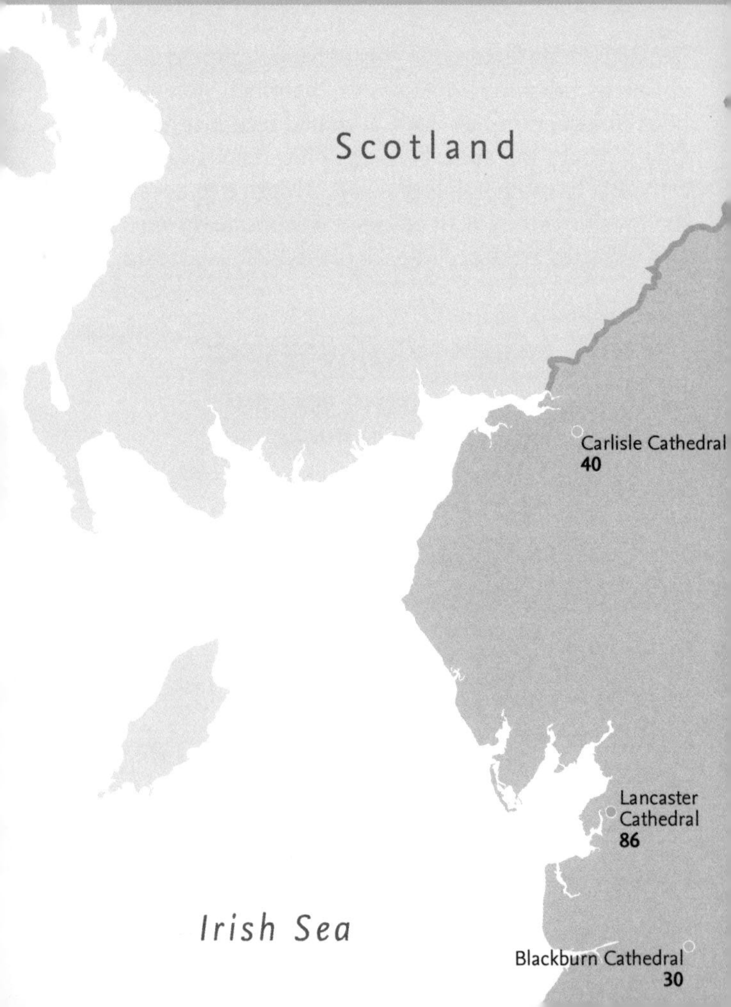
Scotland
Carlisle Cathedral
40
Lancaster
Cathedral
86
Irish Sea
Blackburn Cathedral
30

Numbers in **bold** indicate the page
where the cathedral can be found

North Sea

Newcastle Cathedral
126

Newcastle
Cathedral
130

Durham Cathedral
62

Key
- Church of England cathedral
- Roman Catholic cathedral

Middlesbrough Cathedral
122

England

Ripon Cathedral
164

York Minster
214

Bradford
Cathedral
32

Leeds Cathedral
90

Wakefield Cathedral
200

Central England

Irish
Sea

England

Wales

Ripon Cathedral
164

Lancaster
Cathedral
86

York Minster
214

Bradford
Cathedral
32

Leeds Cathedral
90

Wakefield Cathe
200

Blackburn Cathedral
30

Liverpool Metropolitan
Cathedral 112
Liverpool Cathedral
108

Salford Cathedral
180

Manchester Cathedral
118

Sheffield Cathe
186

Sheffield Cathedral
184

Chester Cathedral
44

Southwell Minster
194

Nottingham Cathedral
144

Derby Cathedral
60

Shrewsbury Cathedral
188

Lichfield Cathedral
98

Leicester Cathedral
94

Birmingham Cathedral
26

Birmingham Cathedral
24

Coventry Cathed
56

Worcester Cathedral
210

Northampton Cathedr.
13

Hereford Cathedral
82

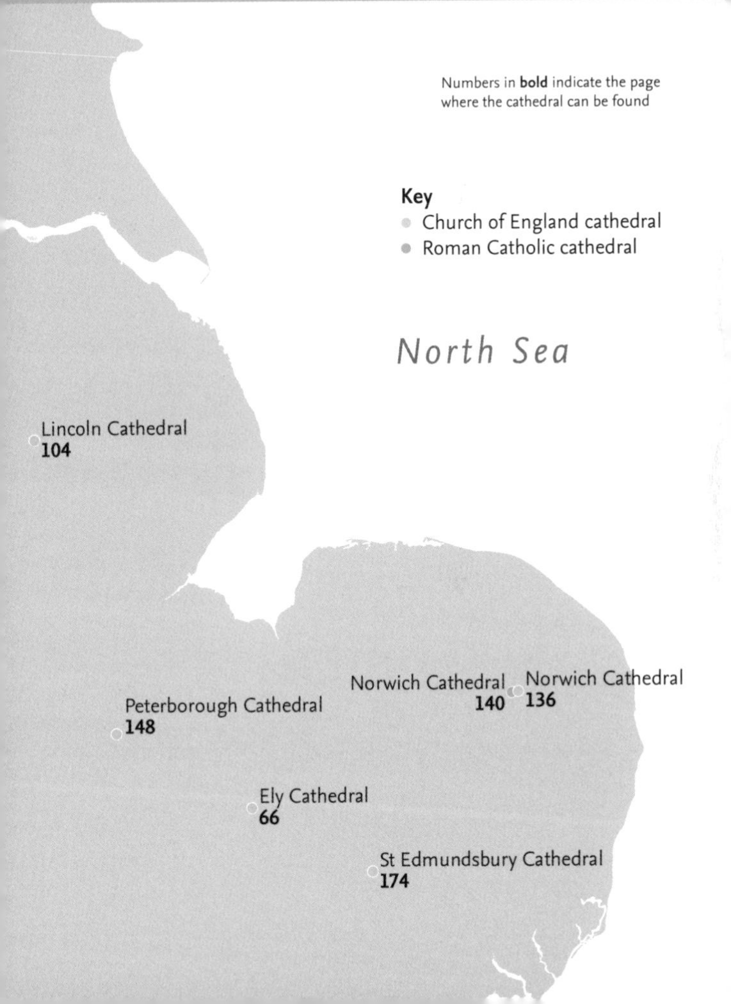

Numbers in **bold** indicate the page
where the cathedral can be found

Key
- Church of England cathedral
- Roman Catholic cathedral

North Sea

Lincoln Cathedral
104

Norwich Cathedral   Norwich Cathedral
140 **136**

Peterborough Cathedral
148

Ely Cathedral
66

St Edmundsbury Cathedral
174

Southern England

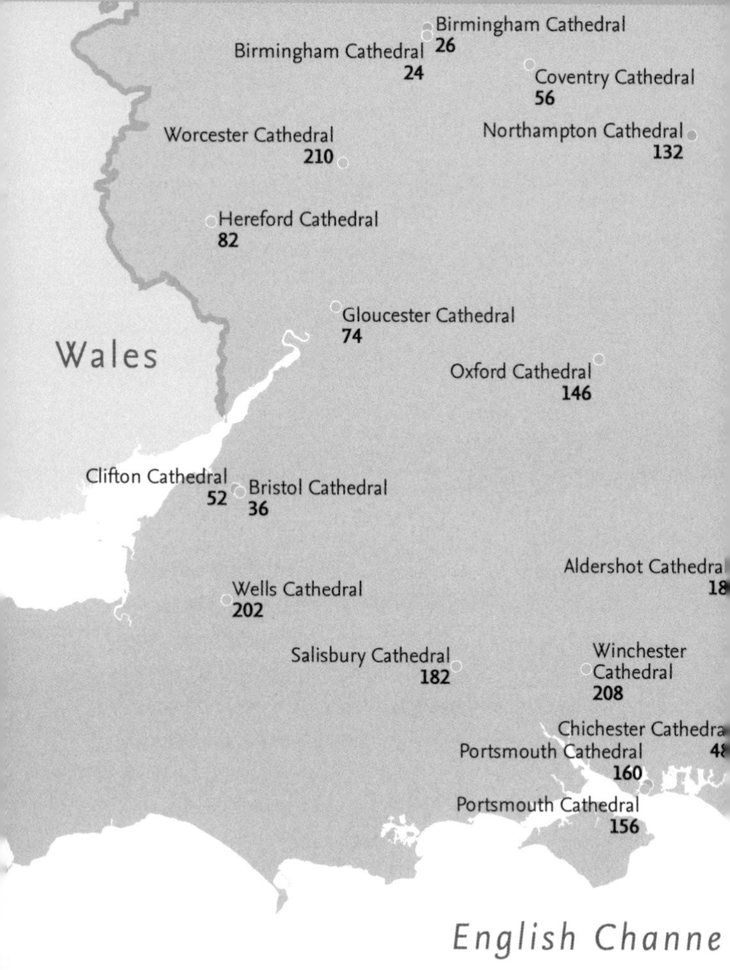
Birmingham Cathedral
26
Birmingham Cathedral
24
Coventry Cathedral
56
Worcester Cathedral
210
Northampton Cathedral
132
Hereford Cathedral
82
Gloucester Cathedral
74
Wales
Oxford Cathedral
146
Clifton Cathedral
52
Bristol Cathedral
36
Aldershot Cathedral
18
Wells Cathedral
202
Salisbury Cathedral
182
Winchester Cathedral
208
Chichester Cathedra
48
Portsmouth Cathedral
160
Portsmouth Cathedral
156
English Channe

Ely Cathedral
66

St Edmundsbury Cathedral
174

England

St Albans Cathedral
172

Chelmsford Cathedral
42

North Sea

St Paul's Cathedral
176

Brentwood Cathedral
34

Westminster
Cathedral
206

Southwark Cathedral **190**
St George's Cathedral
192

Guildford Cathedral
8

Rochester Cathedral
168

Canterbury Cathedral
38

Arundel Cathedral
22

Key

- Church of England cathedral
- Roman Catholic cathedral

Numbers in **bold** indicate the page
where the cathedral can be found

thwest England

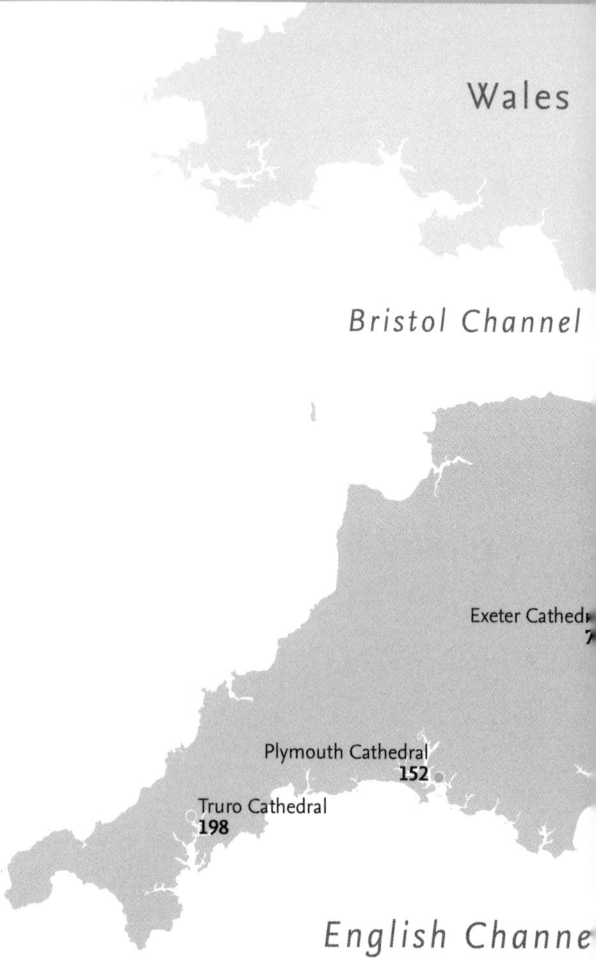
Wales
Bristol Channel
Exeter Cathed
Plymouth Cathedral
152
Truro Cathedral
198
English Channe

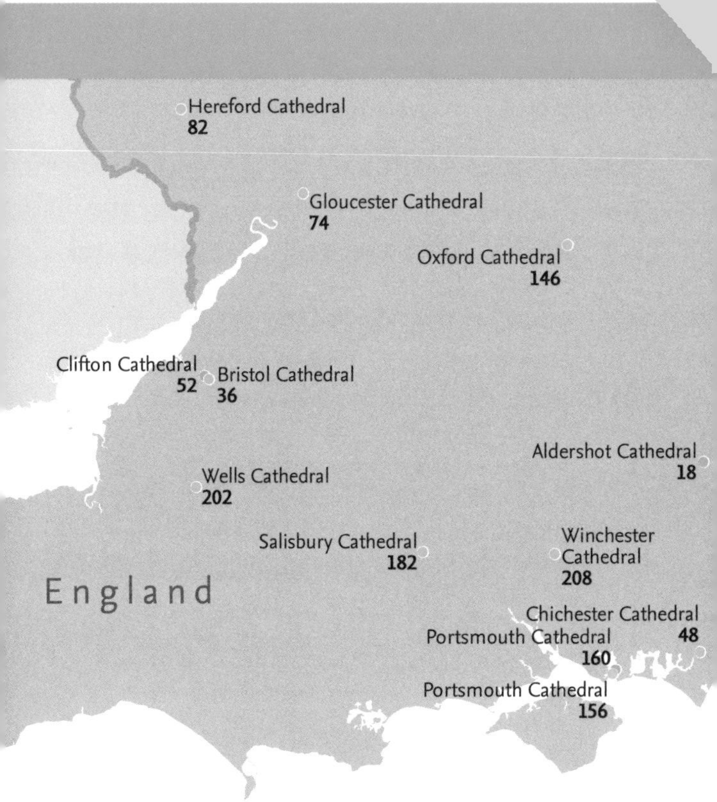

Hereford Cathedral
82

Gloucester Cathedral
74

Oxford Cathedral
146

Clifton Cathedral   Bristol Cathedral
52   **36**

Aldershot Cathedral
18

Wells Cathedral
202

Salisbury Cathedral
182

Winchester
Cathedral
208

England

Chichester Cathedral
Portsmouth Cathedral   **48**
160

Portsmouth Cathedral
156

RC – BISHOPRIC OF THE FORCES

Cathedral Church of St Michael and St George,
Queens Avenue, Aldershot, Hampshire, GU11 2BY
01252 329684 | www.rcbishopricforces.org.uk/cathedral

The Cathedral Church of St Michael and St George
serves as the Roman Catholic cathedral for the Bishopric
of the Forces, which provides chaplains to the British
Armed Forces. The church was designed in 1892 by two
military engineers; Ingers Bell and Aston Webb. It was
originally intended as the principal church for the
Anglican chaplaincies of the British Army and therefore
the ruling British monarch (the 'Supreme Governor of
the Church of England'), Queen Victoria, laid the
cathedral's foundation stone on 27 June 1892 and was
present at the consecration by the Bishop of Winchester
on 7 October 1893.

However, in the early 1970s the number of Catholic soldiers
in the area was on the rise and their previous place of
worship, the Church of St Michael and St Sebastian,
was becoming unsuitable. Since there were other
Church of England churches locally, the cathedral
became the seat of the Roman Catholic Bishop of the
Forces and was dedicated to both St Michael and

St George. Originally dedicated solely to St George, an image of the Saint standing above the slain dragon still resides above the main entrance. Interestingly, several of the stained glass windows do not fit neatly into their frames because they were painstakingly moved from their original home at the Church of St Michael and St Sebastian when it closed in 1973.

: NON : NOBIS : DOMINE : NON : NOB

SEƆ : NOMINI : TVO : ƉA : GLORIAM

Arundel Cathedral

RC – DIOCESE OF ARUNDEL AND BRIGHTON

Cathedral Church of Our Lady and St Philip Howard,
London Road, Arundel, West Sussex, BN18 9AY
01903 882297 | www.arundelcathedral.org

The Cathedral Church of Our Lady and St Philip Howard
was originally dedicated to the Italian St Philip Neri in 1873,
having been established by Henry Fitzalan-Howard,
15th Duke of Norfolk, as the Catholic parish church of
Arundel. Interestingly, Joseph Hansom, inventor of the
Hansom cab, was responsible for the French Gothic
architecture of the church. As Dukes of Norfolk and
Earls of Arundel, the Howard family plays a particularly
prominent part in the history of Arundel and their family
seat is still the nearby castle. Indeed, when the church
was designated a cathedral in 1965 and rededicated to
both Our Lady and St Philip, the dedication was changed
eight years later to Howard ancestor St Philip Howard
(1557–95) who was canonised as a martyr after his
death in the Tower of London.

Birmingham Cathedral

COE – DIOCESE OF BIRMINGHAM

The Cathedral Church of St Philip,
Colmore Row, Birmingham, B3 2QB
0121 262 1840 | www.birminghamcathedral.com

Designed by the English Baroque architect, Thomas Archer, St Philip's was built as a parish church in 1715 to accommodate Birmingham's growing population. The church was built at the highest point in Birmingham, on land provided by local landowners Inge and Elizabeth Phillips. Most churches of the time were dedicated to a prominent saint, however in this instance the Philips family were rewarded for their generosity with a dedication to their namesake saint, the Apostle Philip. Following Birmingham's promotion to city status in 1889 the church became the cathedral seat for the newly formed diocese and Bishop of Birmingham, Charles Gore, in 1905. It is modest in size for a cathedral and at 150 feet long (46 metres). Whilst the cathedral was heavily bombed in 1940 during the Second World War, thankfully Birmingham Civic Society had the forethought to remove and protect the cathedral's precious stained glass windows in the early stages of the war. The windows were replaced during restoration work in 1948.

Birmingham Cathedral

RC – ARCHDIOCESE OF BIRMINGHAM

St Chad's Cathedral,
Cathedral House, St Chad's Queensway,
Birmingham, B4 6EU
0121 236 2251 / 0121 236 5535 |
www.stchadscathedral.org.uk

St Chad's was the first Catholic cathedral to be built in England after the English Reformation, which was initiated in 1534 by King Henry VIII. Designed by the famous Gothic revivalist architect, Augustus Welby Northmore Pugin, it was completed in 1841 and raised to cathedral status in 1850 when Pope Pius IX restored the Catholic hierarchy of England and Wales. Pugin's son and grandson have both added to his work over the years with a memorial spire and chapel respectively.

One hundred years after it was built the cathedral was granted minor basilica status by Pope Pius XII. This allows for the papal coat-of-arms to be placed above the main entrance and use of other symbols designating the cathedral's special relationship with the Pope, such as the scarlet and purple 'cappa parva' worn by the Canons of the Chapter. The cathedral escaped serious damage during the Second World War 'Blitz' of 1940–1 despite a direct hit from a bomb in November 1940. Entering through the roof of the building, the bomb exploded on contact with the cathedral's central heating pipes. Perhaps the work of divine intervention, water from the burst pipes dowsed the flames of the explosion, saving the cathedral from any further damage.

Birmingham Cathedral

Blackburn Cathedral

COE – DIOCESE OF BLACKBURN

Cathedral Church of Blackburn Saint Mary the Virgin
with St Paul
Cathedral Close, Blackburn, BB1 5AA
01254 277430 | www.blackburncathedral.com

This cathedral is one of England's newest cathedrals,
having been elevated to cathedral status in 1926 with the
creation of the Diocese of Blackburn. The existing parish
church of St Mary the Virgin, which was built on the site
in 1826 by Georgian architect John Palmer, now forms
the cathedral's nave.

With the outbreak of the Second World War, plans to
extend the existing building were put on hold. The
impressive additions that make up the building we see
today began in 1938 and were completed in 1977, when
the church was formally consecrated as a cathedral.
It has seen further restoration to blend modern (1960s)
architecture with the earlier structure. The concrete
lantern tower was replaced with natural stone and the east
end roof and parapets rebuilt. The site of the cathedral has
been home to a holy building since the 11th century, with
the 5th Abbot of Whalley, John Lindley, suggesting a link
to Romano-British Christianity as far back as AD 596.

Bradford Cathedral

COE — DIOCESE OF LEEDS

Cathedral Church of St Peter,
1 Stott Hill, Bradford, West Yorkshire, BD1 4EH
01274 777720 | www.bradfordcathedral.org

The Bradford Parish Church of St Peter was elevated to cathedral status in 1919 with the creation of the former Diocese of Bradford, which has now been superseded by the Diocese of Leeds. A site of Christian worship since Anglo-Saxon times, a Norman church was later commissioned by English peeress Alice de Laci before being destroyed by raiding Scots 300 years later in 1327. During the 14th century the church was rebuilt, with the oldest parts of the present building completed in 1458. The church survived the unrest of the 16th-century Reformation and 17th-century English Civil War periods before seeing major renovation in the 18th and 19th centuries as a result of the population boom in the area following the Industrial Revolution. Plans for 20th-century extensions to create a fitting cathedral church were delayed by the First and Second World Wars, with renovations taking place from the 1950s right up until 1987.

Brentwood Cathedral

RC – DIOCESE OF BRENTWOOD

Cathedral Church of St Mary and St Helen,
Clergy House, Ingrave Road, Brentwood, CM15 8AT
01277 265235 | www.cathedral-brentwood.org/blog-2

The Roman Catholic Cathedral Church of St Mary and
St Helen dates from 1861. Originally a parish church
built in a Gothic style, this relatively small building was
elevated to cathedral status in 1917 with the creation
of the Diocese of Brentwood. The church was enlarged
between 1989–91 by architect Quinlan Terry using the
early Italian Renaissance, English Baroque and St Paul's
Cathedral in London as inspiration. Funding for these
enlargements was provided by anonymous donors.
The new cathedral was dedicated on 31 May 1991 by
Cardinal Hume. Interestingly, the terracotta Stations
of the Cross, which can be found on the walls of the
cathedral, may seem familiar to anyone who has ever
used British currency. They were designed by the
Sculptor Raphael Maklouf, who created the image of
Queen Elizabeth II that is used on coins within the UK
and many Commonwealth nations.

Bristol Cathedral

COE – DIOCESE OF BRISTOL

Cathedral Church of the Holy and Undivided Trinity,
College Green, Bristol, BS1 5TJ
0117 926 4879 | bristol-cathedral.co.uk

Founded as St Augustine's Abbey in 1140 by Robert
Fitzharding, 1st Lord Berkeley, the abbey was in the midst
of rebuilding its nave (the central body of the cross-shaped
structure traditional to Romanesque and Gothic Christian
Churches) when Henry VIII dissolved the abbey in 1539
as part of the Dissolution of the Monasteries. Unlike
many abbeys, priories and convents of the time, the
abbey at Bristol survived as one of a group of new
cathedrals created and rededicated by order of Henry as
the 'Supreme Head of the Church in England'. To this
end, in 1542 the abbey became the Cathedral Church of
the Holy and Undivided Trinity and the seat of the bishop
of the new Diocese of Bristol. A rare, surviving example of
a medieval 'hall church', the vaulted ceilings throughout
are all at the same height and the Chapter House and
Abbey Gatehouse both date back to the original 12th-
century abbey. Unfortunately, the cathedral had to make
do without its new nave for the next 300 years until
extensive restoration work took place during the 19th
and 20th centuries.

Canterbury Cathedral

COE – DIOCESE OF CANTERBURY

The Cathedral and Metropolitical Church of Christ
at Canterbury
Cathedral House, 11 The Precincts, Canterbury, CT1 2EH
01227 762862 | www.canterbury-cathedral.org

One of the most famous Christian buildings in England
and the oldest cathedral, Canterbury is the seat of the
Archbishop of Canterbury, leader of the Church of
England and spiritual head of the worldwide Anglican
Community. The cathedral was founded in AD 597 by
Pope Gregory's missionary Augustine, who would
become St Augustine and the first Archbishop of
Canterbury. Augustine was granted a church in
Canterbury by the Anglo-Saxon King Ethelbert who
was the first English king to embrace Christianity.
The site had been used by the Romans as a place of
worship during their occupation of Britain and thus gives
Canterbury the distinction of being the oldest church
in England still in use. The cathedral was completely
rebuilt by the Normans from 1070–7 and again in the
12th century. Canterbury has managed to survive the
English Reformation, Civil War and Second World War
to become the World Heritage Site we see today.

Carlisle Cathedral

COE – DIOCESE OF CARLISLE

The Abbey, Carlisle, Cumbria, CA3 8TZ
01228 548151 | www.carlislecathedral.org.uk

After Oxford Cathedral, Carlisle Cathedral (also known as
the Cathedral Church of the Holy and Undivided Trinity)
is the second smallest of England's ancient cathedrals.
It was founded as an Augustinian monastery in 1122
by it's first Prior (or 'monastic superior') Athelwold.
He would become the first Bishop of Carlisle in 1133
when the monastery was elevated to cathedral status.
Unlike the town's 13th-century friaries, the cathedral
survived Henry VIII's Dissolution of the Monasteries
although it was damaged during the English Civil War
when the nave was destroyed and cathedral stonework
was subsequently taken to fortify nearby Carlisle Castle.
Carlisle Cathedral has experienced various architectural
styles over the years from Norman to Gothic and even
a defensive pele tower. However, it is most famous for
the intricacy of the stained-glass Great East Window.
Originally created around 1350, some of the original
glass still survives and it is thought to be the largest and
most detailed window in England at approx. 23 metres
(76 feet) tall. Even older, although less intricate, is the
12th-century Scandinavian runic 'graffiti', which can still
be seen today.

PRIORS TOWER
RESOURCES CENTRE
ST. CUTHBERT'S CHURCH
TOURIST INFORMATION

NO PARKING

Chelmsford Cathedral

COE – DIOCESE OF CHELMSFORD

The Cathedral of St Mary, St Peter and St Cedd,
Duke Street, Chelmsford, CM1 1EH
01245 294492 | www.chelmsfordcathedral.org.uk

Originally dedicated to St Mary the Virgin, the first
parish church on the site of the present cathedral was
founded, along with the town of Chelmsford itself,
some 800 years ago. Whilst there are elements of
original Norman architecture still visible, major
renovations took place in the 15th century to add the
tower, parapets and porch. Unfortunately, the impact
of the Wars of the Roses meant the renovations took
almost 100 years. Juxtaposed with these more historic
elements are many 20th-century elements such as the
two impressive organs and the south porch's American
window. The American window contains the Stars and
Stripes and the U.S. Air Force coat of arms and was
added in 1953 as a memorial to U.S. forces stationed in
Essex during the Second World War. Chelmsford became
a cathedral and seat of the Bishop of Chelmsford in 1914
when the Diocese of Chelmsford was created.

Chester Cathedral

COE – DIOCESE OF CHESTER

Cathedral Church of Christ and the Blessed Virgin Mary,
St Werburgh Street, Chester, CH1 2DY
01244 324756 | www.chestercathedral.com

Formerly the abbey church of St Werburgh's, a Benedictine
monastery, Chester Cathedral is part of a heritage site
that also includes the former monastic buildings.
However, given Chester's position as a key Roman
settlement it is thought that a basilica may have been
built on the site during the Roman era and there is
certainly evidence of a Saxon chapel dating back to the
10th century. The current cathedral has been modified
many times from its foundation as a monastery in 1093
and includes Romanesque, Norman Gothic and
Georgian styles.

Interestingly, there was already a Cathedral of Chester
when St Werburgh's Abbey was built, albeit briefly.
From 1075 to 1082 the Collegiate Church of St John the
Baptist was the cathedral for the diocese until the area
came under the jurisdiction of the Diocese of Coventry
and Lichfield. Whilst Henry VIII called a halt to the
monastic way of life at Werburgh in 1538, the abbey
became the Church of England Cathedral Church of

Christ and the Blessed Virgin Mary in 1541 by his decree. The former Abbot for the monastery, Thomas Clarke, became the Dean for this new cathedral. Nearly 100 years later, in 1636, part of the south-west tower became home to an ecclesiastical court, which continued to sit until well into the 20th century.

Chester Cathedral

Chichester Cathedral

COE — DIOCESE OF CHICHESTER

Chichester Cathedral, West Street, Chichester,
West Sussex, PO19 1RP
01243 782595 | www.chichestercathedral.org.uk

Chichester Cathedral was not Sussex's first cathedral.
The current cathedral was built to replace the Anglo-
Saxon monastery in nearby Selsey, which was established
in AD 681 when St Wilfrid first brought Christianity to
the area. As was the Norman tradition, existing cathedrals
in more remote locations were relocated to more prominent
towns. The first Norman bishop, Stigand, began work on
a new cathedral in Chichester in 1076 on the site of the
Anglo-Saxon St Peter's Church. The cathedral was finished
in 1108 and consecrated as the Cathedral Church of the
Holy Trinity by Bishop Ralph de Luffa. Interestingly, the
cathedral is notable as being the only English medieval
cathedral that is visible from the sea.

Fire damage in the early and late 12th century meant
that extensive restoration work was necessary, including
the unusual addition of chapels to the sides of the nave,
making Chichester one of the widest cathedrals in England.
Like many other English cathedrals, Chichester was
significantly damaged during the 16th-century English

Reformation and the resulting 17th-century Civil War. For instance, the Shrine of St Richard, an important place of pilgrimage for many Christians, was completely destroyed in 1538 along with the removal of much of the original medieval stained glass. The cathedral library was also extensively damaged a century later, in 1642, by Parliamentary troops. However, despite this neglect a series of restoration works in the 19th, 20th and 21st centuries has seen the replacement of St Richard's Shrine, with an altar dedicated to the Saint, the introduction of Sir George Gilbert Scott's impressive spire, and a significant collection of more modern sculptures, tapestries and stained glass, skilfully blending the old and new.

Chichester Cathedral

Clifton Cathedral

RC — DIOCESE OF CLIFTON

Cathedral Church of Saints Peter and Paul,
Clifton Park, Bristol, BS8 3BX
0117 973 8411 | www.cliftoncathedral.org

One of the most modern Roman Catholic cathedrals in
England, the Cathedral Church of Saints Peter and Paul
was commissioned in 1965 and constructed over a
three-year period before being consecrated on 29 June
1973, the feast day of Saints Peter and Paul. The cathedral
was built to replace Bristol's original Roman Catholic
cathedral, the pro-cathedral of the Holy Apostles.
Building work for the pro-cathedral initially began in
1834 half a mile from the current Clifton Cathedral.
Unfortunately, the hillside location on Park Place meant
that laying foundations was particularly tricky and after a
second attempt to restart the building work in 1843 the
site was left unfinished for another fifteen years before
a roof was added to allow the makeshift cathedral to
be used.

The Diocese of Clifton was created in 1850 with the
intention to build a new cathedral at a new location
within Bristol. However, the pro-cathedral remained in
service until 1973 before becoming a location for the

Steiner School, and more recently being redeveloped into luxury and student accommodation. The unusual design for the current Clifton Cathedral was considered with the congregation in mind. It forms a hexagonal sanctuary with no eye level windows so churchgoers are positioned as close as possible to the focal point of the church; the altar. The triangular position of the altar, Blessed Sacrament Chapel and the baptismal font was also considered with the movement of the congregation to and from the church in mind. Such was the forethought behind the new cathedral that the detailed architectural plans have even been buried under the foundation stone within a copper tube for posterity.

Clifton Cathedral

rebuilding a completely new church, the cathedral community of the time and architect Sir Basil Spence chose to retain the remains as a garden of remembrance alongside a new contemporary building. It was hoped that these contrasting elements of the 'new' cathedral (which would remain known as the Cathedral Church of St Michael) would inspire peace and reconciliation in the aftermath of the war. The new cathedral site opened in 1962 and has been recognised as a post-war architectural landmark ever since, even being voted third of twenty-one iconic British Landmarks of the 21st century by *The Independent* newspaper.

Coventry Cathedral

Derby Cathedral

COE – DIOCESE OF DERBY

Cathedral Church of All Saints,
18–19 Iron Gate, Derby, DE1 3GP
01332 341201 | www.derbycathedral.org

The building previously known as All Saints' Church
became a cathedral and seat for the Bishop of Derby in
1927 with the introduction of the Diocese of Derby the
same year. The original church was said to be founded in
AD 943 by the Anglo-Saxon King Edmund I as a collegiate
church (a training school for priests). However, the current
structure dates mainly from the 18th century when the
vicar of the time, Dr Michael Hutchinson, decided in 1723
that the deteriorating 14th-century version of the building
needed to be demolished and replaced. The 65 metre
(212 feet) tower, which had been added to the cathedral
in the 16th century in a distinctive Perpendicular Gothic
style, was retained alongside the new neo-Classical
building created by architect James Gibbs in 1725. It is
still possible for visitors to climb the tower today and for
keen bell ringers it is worth noting that the cathedral
houses the oldest ring of ten bells in the world. Indeed,
the oldest and largest bell (D-flat) pre-dates the tower
itself and is said to have been relocated from Dale Abbey
following the Dissolution of the Monasteries.

Durham Cathedral

COE – DIOCESE OF DURHAM

Cathedral Church of Christ, the Blessed Virgin Mary
and St Cuthbert,
The College, Durham, DH1 3EH
0191 386 4266 | www.durhamcathedral.co.uk

Founded in 1093 to replace an earlier wooden structure
known as the 'White Church', Durham Cathedral is
regarded as one of the finest examples of Norman
architecture and both the cathedral and nearby Durham
Castle are UNESCO World Heritage Sites. The cathedral
was built as part of a monastic foundation to house the
shrine of Saint Cuthbert of Lindisfarne. After a number
of Viking attacks, the Benedictine monks of Lindisfarne
Priory decided to move the Saint's relics to a safer
location and eventually settled on the hilltop peninsula
on the River Wear at Durham.

The Diocese of Durham was run by the Prince-Bishops
from 1080–1836. In addition to their ecclesiastical duties
they were also granted political and military authority,
with the location of the cathedral and Durham Castle
providing an ideal stronghold for ruling the northern
border areas. Like many other holy buildings of the time,
the monastery was surrendered to Henry VIII in

December 1539 during the Dissolution of the Monasteries. Henry re-founded the cathedral under the rule of the Crown in May 1541, with the previous cathedral Prior becoming Dean and monks from the monastery becoming the first twelve Canons.

The cathedral saw further unrest 100 years later during the English Civil War and even briefly became a holding cell for thousands of Scottish soldiers defeated by Cromwell at the 1650 Battle of Dunbar. There was some attempt to restore the cathedral in the 18th century (with varying success). However, serious conservation did not really begin until the 19th century onwards when the city's other famous institution, Durham University, was founded by the Bishop of Durham.

Durham Cathedral

Ely Cathedral

COE – DIOCESE OF ELY

Cathedral Church of the Holy and Undivided Trinity,
Chapter House, The College, Ely, CB7 4DL
01353 667735 | www.elycathedral.org

St Etheldreda, Anglo-Saxon princess and Northumbrian
virgin Queen, founded an Abbey Church on the site of
the current cathedral around AD 673 having been left the
Isle of Ely as a dower or 'morning gift' by her first husband.
The original abbey was eventually destroyed by Vikings
and re-established as a wealthy Benedictine community
by Ethelwold in AD 970. Following the Siege of Ely, the
abbey was rebuilt as an impressive Norman church in
1083 by Abbot Simeon and dedicated to St Etheldreda
and St Peter. The ninety-year-old Abbot had previously
been a Prior at Winchester Cathedral and the designs
of both cathedrals are very similar, built in the shape of
a cruciform. In 1109 the Diocese of Ely was created and
the church was given cathedral status.

Whilst much of the cathedral survived the Dissolution of
the Monasteries many statues and artefacts were destroyed
including St Etheldreda's Shrine. This was by decree of
Bishop Thomas Goodrich, who had ordered the destruction
of all relics and shrines to Anglo-Saxon saints. In 1541,

under Henry VIII, the cathedral was renamed the Cathedral Church of the Holy and Undivided Trinity and Robert Steward, the former Prior, became the first Dean of the new Chapter. The 17th-century Commonwealth and English Civil War brought further disrepair. Indeed, had Oliver Cromwell and his army not been occupying the Isle of Ely during the 1640s the cathedral may have been completely destroyed. Restoration work in the 18th, 19th and 20th centuries brought the cathedral back to its former glory, retaining impressive Romanesque and decorated gothic features. It continues to be known locally as 'the ship of the Fens' due to its prominent position in the local landscape overlooking the Fenlands, the coastal plains of Eastern England.

Ely Cathedral

Exeter Cathedral

COE — DIOCESE OF EXETER

Cathedral Church of St Peter,
1 The Cloisters, Exeter, EX1 1HS
01392 255573 | www.exeter-cathedral.org.uk

In 1050, the seat of the Bishop of Devon and Cornwall
was moved from nearby Crediton to Exeter due to the
threat of pagan raids from the sea. Regular outdoor
sermons by the then Bishop of Exeter, Leofric, were said
to have taken place at the site of the current cathedral.
However, an existing Saxon church dedicated to Saint
Mary and Saint Peter was used as the Bishop of Exeter's
seat until 1107 when a new Norman Bishop (and
William the Conqueror's nephew), William Warelwast,
was appointed. Plans were made for an impressive
Norman cathedral and foundations were laid in 1133.
However, it was not completed until around 1400 after
a partial rebuild in the more modern Decorated Gothic
style and the inclusion of the impressive, uninterrupted
medieval vaulted ceiling, the longest of its kind in the
world. The cathedral sustained some damage during
the Dissolution of the Monasteries and the Civil War but
was badly hit during the Second World War when Exeter
was specifically targeted by the Luftwaffe during the
1942 'Baedeker Blitz'. The chapel of St James and nearby

walls and aisles were destroyed. Thankfully, the most valuable artefacts and historic documents such as the 10th-century Exeter Book had been removed and stored elsewhere in expectation of a bombing raid. Restoration of the bomb-damaged areas of the cathedral uncovered both Roman and Norman architectural remains.

Exeter Cathedral

Gloucester Cathedral

COE – DIOCESE OF GLOUCESTER

Cathedral Church of the Holy and Indivisible Trinity,
2 College Green, Gloucester, GL1 2LX
01452 528095 | www.gloucestercathedral.org.uk

The origins of the cathedral date from Osric, an Anglo-Saxon prince who founded a religious order on the site in AD 678. The foundations of the present church were laid by Abbot Serlo in 1089 after his appointment from Mont St-Michel in Normandy by William the Conqueror to reverse the fortunes of the floundering monastery. The Abbey of St Peter continued to flourish and expand over the next 500 years under the See of Worcester. It became a shrine to King Edward II when his body was interred there after his suspicious death at nearby Berkeley Castle. The impressive nave centrepiece, crypt, aisles and chapels are all Norman in design, with further additions celebrating various styles of Gothic architecture.

The Abbey surrendered to King Henry VIII in January 1540 and became the seat of the Bishop of Gloucester in 1541, to be run by a Dean and a chapter of Canons as opposed to a monastic community. The cathedral lost its leader in 1555 when Bishop Hooper was burned at the stake by 'Bloody Mary', Catholic daughter of Henry VIII, and the building itself was nearly lost under Oliver Cromwell save for the intervention of the local mayor and other Parliamentarians. Once the monarchy was restored in the 17th century the cathedral prospered and benefitted from major refurbishment in the 19th century. Today it is perhaps most famously recognised by Harry Potter fans as Hogwarts School in *Harry Potter and the Philosopher's Stone.*

Gloucester Cathedral

Guildford Cathedral

COE – DIOCESE OF GUILDFORD

Cathedral Church of the Holy Spirit,
Stag Hill, Guildford, Surrey, GU2 7UP
01483 547860 | www.guildford-cathedral.org

Standing in a commanding position on Stag Hill,
former hunting ground of the kings of England, the
Cathedral Church of the Holy Spirit can be seen for
miles around. The cathedral was originally
commissioned in 1927 following the creation of the
Diocese of Guildford. Construction of the cathedral
began in 1936 under architect Edward Maufe and was
planned to take place over a number of years when
funding allowed. However, the onset of the Second
World War meant that building work was delayed until
1952 and the nearby Holy Trinity Church became
Guildford's temporary cathedral.

Provost Walter Boulton oversaw the 'buy a brick'
fundraising effort for the new cathedral in the 1950s,
which allowed a buyer to sign their name on the brick
they had bought for the sum of 2 shillings and 6 pence
(12 and a half pence in modern currency). The bricks of
two of the most famous donors, Queen Elizabeth II and
Prince Philip, are displayed within the cathedral today.

Guildford Cathedral was finally consecrated on 17 May 1961, making it one of the newest Church of England cathedrals after Liverpool Cathedral.*

Despite Guildford Cathedral's young age, it still contains historical memorials and artefacts. The angel statue that sits atop the 49 metre (160 feet) tower was donated in memory of Sgt Reginald Adgey-Edgar, a casualty of the Second World War in 1944, and the wooden cross marking the site of the new cathedral from 1933 was made from timbers which previously belonged to the 19th-century battleship HMS *Ganges*.

*Building work for Liverpool Cathedral began in 1904 but the building was not completed and consecrated until 1978.

Guildford Cathedral

Hereford Cathedral

COE – DIOCESE OF HEREFORD

Cathedral Church of St Mary the Virgin and St Ethelbert, 5 College Cloisters, Cathedral Close, Hereford, HR1 2NG
01432 374200 | www.herefordcathedral.org

The site of Hereford Cathedral is said to have been a place of Christian worship since the 7th century when a cathedral was founded in the diocese by Putta, 1st Bishop of Hereford. The cathedral is dedicated to Mary, mother of Jesus, and the King of the East Angles, Ethelbert. Ethelbert had sought the hand of King Offa of Mercia's daughter but was cruelly beheaded by the King when he travelled to Herefordshire to visit her in AD 792. Ethelbert's remains were brought to the cathedral and he was canonised as a saint shortly afterwards.

The Mercian nobleman Milfred built a replacement stone cathedral in memory of Ethelbert which remained with a few noted alterations until it was destroyed by the 11th-century king of Wales, Gruffydd ap Llywelyn. Saint Ethelbert's shrine was decimated at the same time. A new shrine to the Saint was installed in 2007.

The cathedral was rebuilt by the Normans in the 12th century and the bishop's chapel of today's cathedral dates back to this time. From the 14th century the cathedral was home to the remains of another Saint, 45th Bishop of Hereford Thomas Cantilupe, and was extended and redecorated for this purpose including the famous 'ballflower' of the central tower. Sadly, much of Saint Thomas' shrine and it's treasures were destroyed in 1538 during the Protestant Reformation led by King Henry VIII. The cathedral was later captured by Parliamentary forces during the 17th-century English Civil War and narrowly avoided being deconsecrated. Major restoration work took place in the 19th century and today Hereford Cathedral houses many surviving medieval treasures. These include the Mappa Mundi, a UNESCO listed map of the world dating back to the 13th century, Hereford's Magna Carta and the Hereford Gospels, which date back to the 8th century. In 1996 Queen Elizabeth II opened a new library at the cathedral to house these and other important artefacts.

Hereford Cathedral

Lancaster Cathedral

RC – DIOCESE OF LANCASTER

Cathedral Church of St Peter,
Balmoral Road, Lancaster, LA1 3BT
01524 384820 | www.lancastercathedral.org.uk

Despite fines and punishments for practising Catholics, the faith remained popular in the north west of England in the 17th and 18th centuries. When the Roman Catholic Relief Act was passed in 1791 it allowed new Catholic churches to be built and Lancaster's Catholic community were able to move from their makeshift chapels to a new purpose-built church on Dalton Square, now known as Palatine Hall.

Fifty years later the community had outgrown the church and were also in need of a school, cemetery and convent. Land was purchased not far from the existing Dalton Square church and St Peter's Catholic Church was designed by Lancastrian architect Edward Graham Paley in the style of 13th- and 14th-century (pre-Reformation) English Gothic Catholic churches. Funded primarily by wealthy local Catholic families, the impressive church and its 73 metre (240 foot) spire were built from 1857–9 and consecrated on 4 October 1859. Further additions such as the sacristy, baptistery, stained glass and a new altar were built over the next fifty years. When the Diocese of Lancaster was founded in 1924 to oversee Lancashire, Cumberland and Westmorland St Peter's Church was seen as the ideal choice for the Bishop's seat.

Lancaster Cathedral

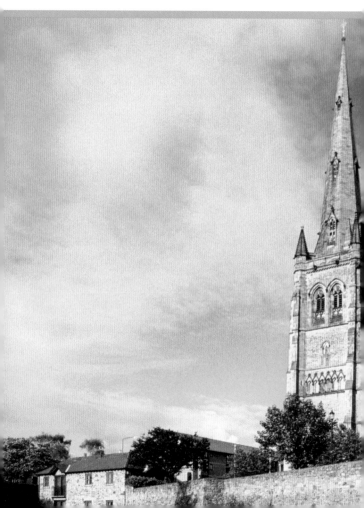

Leeds Cathedral

RC – DIOCESE OF LEEDS

Saint Anne's Cathedral,
Great George Street, Leeds, LS2 8BE
0113 245 4545 | www.dioceseofleeds.org.uk/cathedral

The current cathedral building was completed in 1904. However, Catholicism was not new to Leeds in the post-Reformation era even though the religion had been suppressed and the Catholic population across England had dwindled. In 1786, local cotton spinner and prominent Catholic Joseph Holdsforth successfully petitioned the Vicar of Leeds for a space dedicated to Catholic worship within the city. It would be the first such space since the Reformation. Holdsforth and Father Albert Underhill, a Dominican priest, established a Catholic Mission in a room next door to the Pack Horse Hotel on Briggate, a busy street running from the north to the south of the town. Following the Roman Catholic Relief Act of 1791, St Mary's Chapel was built in nearby Lady Lane in October 1794.

The Industrial Revolution swelled the population of Leeds dramatically over the next fifty years, including a significant number of Irish Catholic workers who initially arrived to fill the mills and quarries and later came to escape the Potato Famine. To accommodate this larger Catholic community, St Patrick's Catholic Church was established on the outskirts of Leeds in 1831. In 1836, the current priest at St Mary's Chapel, Father Henry Walmsley, found a more central site for a larger, replacement church and St Anne's Church was opened on Great George Street in October 1838. This was the same year in which Leeds received its first Roman Catholic mayor; James Holdsforth, a relation of Joseph.

When the Diocese of Leeds was created in 1878 St Anne's Church became a cathedral. However, twenty years later the cathedral was compulsorily purchased and demolished by the Leeds Corporation to allow for redevelopment of the surrounding area. The current cathedral was built from 1901–4 a short walk from St Anne's by architect John Henry Eastwood. It was designed in the Arts and Crafts neo-Gothic style to maximise the limited space available in such a central location. Unlike many other English cities, there is no Church of England cathedral in Leeds since the Anglican diocese of Leeds is supported by cathedrals in Ripon, Wakefield and Bradford.

Leeds Cathedral

Leicester Cathedral

COE – DIOCESE OF LEICESTER

Cathedral Church of St Martin,
St Martins House, 7 Peacock Lane, Leicester, LE1 5PZ
0116 261 5200 | leicestercathedral.org

Leicester had its own Saxon bishop and Christianity had
arrived in the area with the Romans, who referred to the
town as *Ratae*. However, the original diocese of Leicester
was no longer in existence by the 9th century and both
the town and parish church fell under the jurisdiction
of Lincoln and then Peterborough. It was not until 1926
that a new diocese of Leicester was created, and the
Church of St Martin was elevated to cathedral status
in 1927.

The cathedral building we see today is mainly Gothic in
style although it has had several reincarnations since the
Normans built a church on the site in 1086 dedicated to
the 4th-century saint Martin of Tours.

The church survived the Reformation of the 16th century
with little significant damage although some of the internal
artefacts were removed. It has since been subject to
many restoration projects, most significantly in the
1860s when Victorian architect John Raphael Rodrigues

Brandon completely rebuilt the tower, spire and nave roof. St George's Chapel was reconstructed in 1921 as a memorial to the soldiers of the Royal Leicestershire Regiment who lost their lives in the First World War. Local soldiers killed in the Crimean, South African and Second World War are also recorded here in remembrance.

In 2015 the remains of King Richard III (1452–85) were interred at the cathedral in the newly created Chapel of Christ the King having been discovered underneath a nearby car park within the ruins of the former Greyfriars Church. Richard had been buried there with little pomp and ceremony after his death at the Battle of Bosworth Field. He was the last English king to die in battle and the last Yorkist King from the House of Plantagenet. Fittingly, the coffin marking his final resting place was crafted by a direct relation of his elder sister, Anne of York.

Leicester Cathedral

Lichfield Cathedral

COE – DIOCESE OF LICHFIELD

Cathedral Church of the Blessed Virgin Mary
and St Chad,
19A The Close, Lichfield, Staffordshire, WS13 7LD
01543 306100 | www.lichfield-cathedral.org

In AD 666 St Chad, Bishop of Mercia, declared
'Lyccidfelth' his bishop's seat and Lichfield became the
focal point of Christianity in the Kingdom of Mercia,
now known as the Midlands. Whilst the bishop's seat
was moved to Chester in the 11th century in the
aftermath of a Viking attack, Lichfield remained a place
of pilgrimage for many years after Chad's death in
AD 672. A Saxon church was erected as a resting place
for his remains, followed by the construction of a
Norman cathedral in 1085.

The construction of the Norman cathedral was overseen
by Bishop Roger de Clinton, who fortified the building
and surrounding town against attack with a bank, ditch
and entrance gates. In 1195, the bishop's seat returned
to Lichfield and work began on an ornate Gothic cathedral
that took 150 years to complete. This third incarnation
with its three impressive spires is, for the most part, the
same Lichfield Cathedral we see today.

However, the cathedral has had a tumultuous history. During the Reformation the shrine to St Chad was removed, altars and adornment were destroyed, and the cathedral became a solemn, sombre place. The English Civil War skirmishes during 1642–51 brought further hardships. The city was split between allegiances to King Charles I and his Royalists and the Parliamentarians or 'Roundheads', with the authorities on the side of the King and the townspeople in support of Parliament. Initially, the cathedral was under Royalist occupation before being taken over by the Parliamentarians in 1643. Lord Robert Brooke, the Parliamentarian leader in charge of the assault, was fatally shot in the left eye by a deaf and dumb lookout atop the cathedral's central spire named John Dyott who had spotted his vibrant, purple officer's uniform. Brooke's death was considered a good omen by the Royalists holding the cathedral since it happened on 2 March, which was also St Chad's Day. Unfortunately, the cathedral was badly damaged in the battle to take control and its central spire was destroyed. Parliamentarian occupation saw even further damage as monuments were destroyed, statues were defaced, and parts of the cathedral were used as animal pens. It would be many years before the building would be restored to its former glory.

Lichfield Cathedral

More recently, in 2003, the remains of an early Saxon statue of what is believed to be Archangel Gabriel were discovered during restoration work. Historians believe this to be part of the coffin that contained the bones of St Chad, whose followers saved him from the Viking attack which decimated Mercia in the 9th century and the violence of the Reformation 700 years later.

Lichfield Cathedral

Lincoln Cathedral

COE – DIOCESE OF LINCOLN

Cathedral Church of the Blessed Virgin Mary
of Lincoln,
Lincoln Cathedral, Minster Yard, Lincoln, LN2 1PX
01522 561600 | lincolncathedral.com

Benedictine Monk Remigius de Fécamp, the first Bishop
of Lincoln, moved the episcopal seat to Lincoln in 1072
and commenced construction of the Cathedral Church of
the Blessed Virgin Mary. The cathedral was consecrated
twenty years later, two days after Remigius' death in
1092. Within the first 100 years of its life, the cathedral
suffered destruction from fire and the largest earthquake
ever felt in the UK (on 15 April 1185). As a result of the
earthquake, only the western side of the original
building remains today.

Over the next 500 years the cathedral saw significant
restoration and expansion. The French Bishop Hugh
de Burgundy of Avalon, who was later canonised as
St Hugh of Lincoln, rebuilt the cathedral in the Early
English Gothic style. Pointed arches, flying buttresses
and ribbed vaulting were added later as was the
architectural style of the time. The cathedral was
expanded in the 13th century by agreement of the

current monarch, Henry III, to allow for more visitors to the Shrine of St Hugh. When the Queen Consort of Edward I, Eleanor of Castile, died in 1290 near Lincoln her internal organs were interred at the cathedral in a tomb identical to the Westminster Abbey tomb where her body was buried. The Queen's heart was buried separately alongside the heart of her son Alphonso in the Dominican priory at Blackfriars in London.

In the early 14th century the height of the cathedral was raised. A wooden spire was added to the central tower in 1311 bringing the tower to an impressive 160 metres (525 feet) high. This made the cathedral the tallest structure in the world, even taller than the Great Pyramid of Giza, which had been the tallest structure up to that point for nearly 4,000 years. Unfortunately, the spire was lost two centuries later during a storm in 1549. Over the years the cathedral has also housed a number of precious artefacts in its impressive libraries. This includes the text of the saint and scholar the Venerable Bede and the Lincoln copy of the Magna Carta which was signed by the 13th-century Bishop of Lincoln, Hugh of Wells, although this has now been moved to Lincoln Castle.

Lincoln Cathedral

Liverpool Cathedral

COE – DIOCESE OF LIVERPOOL

Cathedral Church of Christ,
Liverpool Cathedral, St James' Mount, Liverpool, L1 7AZ
0151 702 7217 | www.liverpoolcathedral.org.uk

The Church of England diocese of Liverpool was founded
in 1880 but had no formal cathedral initially, only an
unsuitably small parish church dedicated to St Peter
which served as the pro-cathedral. A site for a new
cathedral was agreed in 1885 but was later abandoned
when it was also deemed too small. Members of the
diocesan clergy also disagreed amongst themselves as to
whether a new cathedral was needed given the expense
it would bring. Therefore, it was not until 1902 that the
site at St James' Mount was purchased and plans made
to demolish St Peters Church to sell the land as a
contribution to the cost of the new cathedral.

Competition to design the new cathedral was fierce since
it would be only the third Anglican cathedral to be built
since the Reformation (after the rebuilt St Paul's Cathedral
and Truro Cathedral). The successful applicant was
English architect Sir Giles Gilbert Scott, a twenty-two-
year-old architectural student, whose designs combined
Gothic tradition with modernism.

Although the foundation stone was laid by King Edward VII in 1904, the building of Liverpool's Cathedral Church of Christ was delayed first through design and redesign issues, and then still further by two World Wars. A service of dedication was finally held in October 1978, seventy-four years after the initial building work was begun and eighteen years after Scott's death. England's newest* Church of England cathedral is also its largest, at an impressive 188.7 metres (619 feet) in length and 9,687.4 sq. metres (104,275 sq. feet) in area.

There are two cathedrals in Liverpool; the Church of England Cathedral Church of Christ and the Roman Catholic Metropolitan Cathedral of Christ the King. The cathedrals are just over half a mile apart and, fittingly, the street which joins the two sites is called Hope Street. However, this is by coincidence rather than design as the street takes it name from local resident William Hope who predates both cathedrals.

*Building work commenced for Guildford Cathedral in 1936, however, it was finished and consecrated in 1961.

Liverpool Cathedral

Liverpool Metropolitan Cathedral

Metropolitan Cathedral of Christ the King,
Cathedral House, Mount Pleasant, Liverpool, L3 5TQ
0151 709 9222 | www.liverpoolmetrocathedral.org.uk

Liverpool Metropolitan Cathedral is not only the mother
church of the Roman Catholic Diocese of Liverpool, it is
also the seat of the Archbishop of Liverpool, the leader
of the Catholic Church in the North West of England
and the Isle of Man.

Prior to the 16th-century Reformation, there was no
cathedral in Liverpool. The area fell variously under the
Diocese of Lichfield, Lichfield and Coventry or Chester.
From the 16th to the mid-19th centuries it was forbidden
to practice openly as a Catholic. In 1850 the Catholic
hierarchy in England was re-established. As a result, the
archdiocese of Westminster and thirteen sees were
created, including the diocese of Liverpool.

With the influx of Irish Catholics to Liverpool as a result
of the Industrial Revolution and the Famine, a Catholic
cathedral was deemed necessary. Initially, Edward Welby
Pugin (1833–75), son of famous architect Augustus

Welby Northmore Pugin, was commissioned to design the new cathedral and a Lady Chapel was created in the grounds of St Edward's College in Everton. Unfortunately, the diocese needed to redirect its financial support to parish churches, schools and orphanages so further plans for the new cathedral were put on hold. The Lady Chapel became the parish church of Our Lady Immaculate until it became structurally unsafe and was demolished in the 1980s.

In 1930 the site of the former Brownlow Hill workhouse infirmary was purchased with the intention to build the new cathedral there. Sir Edwin Lutyens was commissioned to provide a further design. If built to his design, the cathedral would have become the second-largest church in the world after St Peter's Basilica in Vatican City and a suitable counterpart for the neo-Gothic Anglican cathedral being built at the other end of Hope Street by Giles Gilbert Scott. Building work began in June 1933. In 1941, the restrictions of the Second World War and rising costs from £3–£27 million forced construction to stop. Work eventually re-commenced on the crypt, which was finished in 1958 before Lutyens' costly design was abandoned entirely.

Liverpool Metropolitan Cathedral

The present cathedral was designed by Sir Frederick Gibberd. Construction took place over Lutyens' crypt between October 1962 and May 1967 but soon after its opening the cathedral began to exhibit architectural flaws. This led to the cathedral authorities suing Sir Frederick for £1.3 million.

Liverpool Metropolitan Cathedral

Manchester Cathedral

COE – DIOCESE OF MANCHESTER

Cathedral and Collegiate Church of St Mary,
St Denys and St George,
Victoria Street, Manchester, M3 1SX
0161 833 2220 | www.manchestercathedral.org

The Cathedral and Collegiate Church of St Mary, St Denys and St George was extensively restored and extended during the Victorian era, and then again after severe bomb damage during the 1940 Manchester 'Blitz', giving the cathedral a deceptively modern appearance. It actually dates back to the Saxon era, and during 19th-century renovation work the *Angel Stone* was found within one of the original 13th-century walls of the cathedral. The carving is believed to date back to around AD 700 when Manchester's first church was built.

When the initial church was destroyed by Vikings, King Edward the Elder built St Mary's church in AD 923, as noted in the Doomsday Book. Nearly 300 years later, in 1215, the present cathedral was built next to the Baron's Manor House (now Chetham's Music School on Long Millgate). The house was owned by the Norman Gresle family and the current Lord of Manchester, Robert de Gresle.

In 1421 the church became a Collegiate Foundation dedicated to St Mary, St Denys and St George. Sixty years later, James Stanley (uncle by marriage to Henry Tudor, the first of the Tudor Dynasty), became Warden of the Collegiate Church. Over the next 100 years after the Tudor victory at the Battle of Bosworth Field, the cathedral saw many enhancements. This included the famous consort of Minstrel Angels commissioned by Henry Tudor's mother Margaret Beaufort and a number of new chapel buildings.

In 1547 the college was dissolved and all precious artefacts and memorials were removed by either Henry VIII or his son Edward VI. However, Henry's daughter Mary I swiftly reinstated the college when she came to power in 1553 as part of her efforts to reverse the Reformation. Following Civil War damage in 1649, the church saw a series of renovations over the next 200 years before the Diocese of Manchester was created in 1847 and the church became a cathedral. Despite many renovations and extensions, the main body of the cathedral still largely derives from the 13th-century parish church and the coat of arms used by the Gresle family remains visible on the cathedral today.

Manchester Cathedral

Middlesbrough Cathedral

The Cathedral Church of Saint Mary the Virgin,
Dalby Way, Coulby Newham, Middlesbrough, TS8 0TW
01642 597750 | middlesbroughrccathedral.org

Middlesbrough's Roman Catholic cathedral is a modern,
light structure specifically designed to involve the
congregation in active participation, as decreed for new
cathedral buildings by the Second Vatican Council in the
1960s. Building commenced in 1985 and the cathedral
was consecrated in 1998. However, it is not the first
Catholic cathedral in Middlesbrough. An earlier
cathedral on another site in the city had served the
Catholic community since 1879.

The Cathedral Church of Our Lady Of Perpetual Succour
was built on Sussex Street between 1876–8. It was built
as a replacement for the parish church of St Mary's
Chapel, which had become unsuitable for the growing
Catholic population of Middlesbrough. The cathedral
initially fell under the Diocese of Beverley until the
diocese of Middlesbrough was created in 1878. The first
Bishop of Middlesbrough, Richard Lacy, arrived in 1879.

The Sussex Street Cathedral served the community well until the 1970s when the post-war rehousing scheme saw members of the community transferred to other areas of Middlesbrough and new parishes established. It was therefore decided that a new cathedral should be built in Coulby Newham where much of the Catholic community had settled. In the summer of 1984 it was also discovered that the current cathedral on Sussex Street was suffering from structural issues and may be rendered unsafe, expediting plans for the new cathedral. Sadly, the previous cathedral was destroyed by a fire in May 2000 and the remnants of the building had to be demolished shortly afterwards.

Middlesbrough Cathedral

Newcastle Cathedral

COE – DIOCESE OF NEWCASTLE

The Cathedral Church of St Nicholas,
St Nicholas Square, Newcastle upon Tyne, NE1 1PF
0191 232 1939 | stnicholascathedral.co.uk

The Cathedral Church of St Nicholas is named after the patron saint of sailors and boats, a likely result of the cathedral's position north of the River Tyne.

The cathedral was initially built in 1091 as a parish church under the diocese of Durham, shortly after William the Conqueror's son Robert Curthose built the nearby castle for which the city is named. The original Norman building was razed by a fire in 1216 and the current structure replaced it in the 1350s. It was built in the Perpendicular architectural style that was popular at the time. One hundred years later, in 1448, the church's renowned lantern spire was created and acted as a guiding beacon to ships navigating the River Tyne.

Having survived the Reformation unscathed, the church was desecrated by the Scottish Covenanter forces who invaded during the Second Bishops' War of 1640 and later during the First English Civil War of 1644. Major restoration work took place in the 18th century. In the

19th century the population boom resulting from the Industrial Revolution necessitated a new diocese. In 1882 the Diocese of Newcastle was created and the church became the city's new cathedral.

There are two cathedrals in Newcastle, the Church of England Cathedral Church of St Nicholas and the Roman Catholic Cathedral Church of St Mary. St Mary's was the first cathedral to be established in Newcastle, thirty-two years before the creation of the Cathedral Church of St Nicholas.

Newcastle Cathedral

Newcastle Cathedral

RC – DIOCESE OF HEXHAM AND NEWCASTLE

St Mary's Cathedral,
Clayton Street West, Newcastle Upon Tyne, NE1 5HH
0191 232 6953 | www.stmaryscathedral.org.uk

The Roman Catholic Cathedral Church of St Mary was designed by renowned Victorian architect Augustus Welby Northmore Pugin who was responsible for the internal design of the Houses of Parliament. The Cathedral was built in the neo-Gothic style of architecture championed by Pugin between 1842 and 1844. It was funded by the many halfpenny contributions of the immigrant Catholic community on Tyneside. Donations from the prominent Dunn family paid for further enhancements such as the needle spire and the stained glass windows, which include memorials to the family.

The church gained the status of cathedral in 1850 when the Catholic hierarchy was restored by Pope Pius IX and the diocese of Hexham (later changed to the diocese of Hexham and Newcastle) was created. In 2002, Queen Elizabeth II opened the monument dedicated to Cardinal Basil Hume in the cathedral garden.

Northampton Cathedral

RC – DIOCESE OF NORTHAMPTON

Cathedral Church of Our Lady and
St Thomas of Canterbury,
Primrose Hill, Northampton, NN2 6AG
01604 714556 | northamptoncathedral.org

Christianity arrived in Northampton during the Saxon
era. Franciscan churches, abbeys and friaries could be
found across the city from the 5th century until the
Reformation when Northampton became a centre for
Puritan worship. It was not until the 19th century that
Catholicism was once again practiced openly in
Northampton, when Father William Foley opened
St Andrew's chapel on 25 October 1825.

In 1840, William Wareing, the first Bishop of Northampton,
asked renowned Victorian architect Augustus Welby
Northmore Pugin to create a collegiate chapel dedicated
to St Felix. The chapel would sit next to St Andrew's Chapel
to accommodate the growing Catholic community.

In 1864, the next Bishop, Francis Kerril Amherst, asked
Pugin's son Edward to create an extension to the
chapel to make it a suitable cathedral for the Diocese
of Northampton, which had been created in 1850.

This extension, dedicated to Our Lady Immaculate and St Thomas of Canterbury, now forms the nave of today's cathedral and is the final resting place for Bishop Amherst.

The cathedral remained in this slightly unusual composition of different buildings for nearly 100 years until the foundations became unsteady and Bishop Leo Parker called for further renovations. This involved the demolition of Augustus Pugin's original chapel and the introduction of a new central chancel, tower and gallery adjoining the nave built by Edward Pugin. The Blessed Sacrament Altar from St Andrew's was retained and moved to the Blessed Sacrament Chapel. Bishop Parker was buried in the Blessed Sacrament Chapel following his death in 1975.

In 1998, in celebration of the coming millennium, a new stained glass window was added to the Blessed Sacrament Chapel and the layout of the cathedral was reorganised to include a new bishop's throne and elaborate carving entitled *Triptych*. Meaning 'threefold', the carving refers to the Holy Spirit, the Word of God and the Sacrament.

Northampton Cathedral

Norwich Cathedral

COE – DIOCESE OF NORWICH

Cathedral Church of Holy and Undivided Trinity,
65 The Close, Norwich, NR1 4DH
01603 218300 | www.cathedral.org.uk

Norfolk has been part of a Christian diocese since AD 672, when Theodore of Tarsus, Archbishop of Canterbury, created two dioceses within East Anglia. These two diocese were the diocese of Elmham, covering Norfolk, and the diocese of Dunwich. By the 9th century there remained only one diocese, Elmham. This was swiftly relocated to the more urban Thetford by the Normans before becoming the diocese of Norwich in 1094. Dedicated to the Holy and Undivided Trinity, Norwich Cathedral was built between 1096–1145 by Herbert de Losinga, first Bishop of Norwich. An earlier Saxon settlement and two churches were demolished to make room for the extensive cathedral footprint.

The layout remains largely unchanged despite a number of extensions and renovations throughout the medieval period. The tower we see today dates back to Norman times and its spire, the second-tallest in England after Salisbury, has remained in place since 1480. The two-storey cloister, or walkway, is the only one of its kind in England.

It took 133 years to complete, from 1297–1430, after Norwich was hit with the Black Death pandemic.

The cathedral faced a few natural disasters throughout the centuries such as lightning and hurricane damage, but man-made damage was much more wide-reaching. The Tombland riot of 1272, Civil War mobs of 1643 and Second World War bombing offensives left the cathedral in need of extensive restoration. Indeed, an extended period of restoration took place for over fifty years from 1952–2010.

There are two cathedrals in Norwich, the Church of England Cathedral Church of the Holy and Undivided Trinity and the Roman Catholic Cathedral Church of St John the Baptist. However, the Cathedral Church of the Holy and Undivided Trinity predates the Cathedral Church of St John the Baptist by nearly 800 years.

Norwich Cathedral

RC – DIOCESE OF EAST ANGLIA

The Cathedral Church of St John the Baptist,
Unthank Road, Norwich, NR2 2PA
01603 624615 | www.sjbcathedral.org.uk

The Cathedral Church of St John the Baptist is the
second largest Roman Catholic cathedral in England
after Westminster Cathedral. It was constructed between
1882 and 1910 as a parish church on the site of the
former Norwich City Gaol using the designs of architect
George Gilbert Scott Junior, also known as 'Middle Scott'
in reference to his father and two sons who were also
prominent architects.

The Church of St John the Baptist was built in the
Victorian Gothic Revival style and was a gift to the
Catholic Community of Norwich from Henry Fitzalan-
Howard, 15th Duke of Norfolk, in celebration of his
marriage to Lady Flora Abney-Hastings. It is thought to
have been the largest parish church in the country before
being consecrated as the cathedral for the newly formed
Diocese of East Anglia in 1976. Today, it is possible for
visitors to climb the 280 steps of the cathedral tower to
experience a panoramic view of the city.

Norwich Cathedral

Nottingham Cathedral

RC – DIOCESE OF NOTTINGHAM

Cathedral Church of St Barnabas,
North Circus Street, Nottingham, NG1 5AE
0115 953 9839 | www.stbarnabascathedral.org.uk

Designed by renowned architect Augustus Welby
Northmore Pugin, the Roman Catholic Church of
St Barnabas was built between 1841–4. The Church was
built at the behest of Father Robert Wilson, parish priest at
the Church of St John the Evangelist, Nottingham's only
Catholic Church at that point. A new church was needed
because of a surge in numbers in the Catholic Community.

John Talbot, 16th Earl of Shrewsbury and influential
Catholic peer and aristocrat, funded much of the new
cathedral. It was built in the Early English Plain Gothic
style, apart from the ornate Blessed Sacrament Chapel.
The Chapel was seemingly a forerunner of Pugin's move
to the Decorated Gothic style of architecture favoured
in his later designs.

The Church of St Barnabas was raised to cathedral status
in 1852 following the restoration of the Catholic hierarchy
by Pope Pius IX in 1850.

Oxford Cathedral

COE – DIOCESE OF OXFORD

The Cathedral Church of Christ,
Christ Church, University of Oxford,
St Aldates, Oxford, OX1 1DP
01865 276150 | www.chch.ox.ac.uk/cathedral

Christ Church Cathedral is the cathedral for the Diocese
of Oxford. Unusually for a Church of England cathedral
it is also the chapel of Christ Church, a college of the
University of Oxford. Originally Cardinal Thomas Wolsey,
King Henry VIII's chief advisor, began to build his new
'Cardinal College' on the site of the church of St Frideswide's
Priory in 1522 as part of the Renaissance movement to
improve education. However, when Wolsey fell from
grace in 1529 Henry VIII took over the college. In 1532
it was renamed *Aedes Christi*, the House (or Church) of
Christ, and in addition to a place of learning it also
became the cathedral church for the newly created
diocese of Oxford.

After the Restoration of the monarchy in 1660 when
Charles II came to the throne the 'Tom Quad' was created.
The quadrangle linked the hall, cathedral and canonries of
the site and included the bell tower known as Tom Tower,
built to the design of Sir Christopher Wren in 1682.

Peterborough Cathedral

COE – DIOCESE OF PETERBOROUGH

Cathedral Church of St Peter, St Paul and St Andrew, Peterborough, PE1 1XS
01733 355315 | www.peterborough-cathedral.org.uk

Whilst there is archaeological evidence to suggest an even earlier Roman monument, we know that there has been a religious structure on the site of Peterborough Cathedral since at least AD 665. At this time, Peada and Wulfhere, sons of the Saxon King Penda of Mercia, founded a monastery named Medeswell (later changed to Medehamstede: 'the home/farmstead in the water meadows'). Although the Kingdom of Mercia was predominantly pagan the monastery was built as a result of a marriage contract with nearby Christian Northumbria.

The replacement monastic church which forms much of the current cathedral was built between 1118 and 1238 following extensive fire damage to both the monastery and the town after a local bakery caught fire in 1116. Amazingly, the wooden ceiling of the nave survived unharmed and remains in place today, the only one of its kind in England and one of only four surviving examples in Europe. During this period both Henry II and King John visited the monastery, the latter leaving behind what is thought to be a draft copy of the Magna Carta; 'the Black Book of Peterborough'.

Peterborough retained strong links with the monarchy over the next few hundred years. Indeed Catherine of Aragon, first wife of Henry VIII, and Mary Queen of Scots were both buried here, although Mary was later moved to Westminster Abbey. In 1541, Henry created his new Diocese of Peterborough and established the monastic church as a cathedral. The previous abbot, John Chambers, became the first bishop.

Unfortunately this royalist link did not bode well during the English Civil War when Peterborough fell to Oliver Cromwell in 1643. Much of the interior was demolished or destroyed until extensive renovations restored the cathedral to its former glory 200 years later. More recently, the cathedral has undergone major restoration as a result of fire damage in 2001.

Peterborough Cathedral

Plymouth Cathedral

RC – DIOCESE OF PLYMOUTH

The Cathedral Church of St Mary and St Boniface,
45 Cecil Street, Plymouth, Devon, PL1 5HW
01752 662537 | www.plymouthcathedral.co.uk

The Cathedral Church of St Mary and St Boniface was
designed by the architect (and creator of the eponymous
'Hansom Cab') Joseph Hansom and his brother Charles.
It first opened for Mass on 25 March 1858, and was
consecrated in September 1880, following the
introduction of the new Catholic Diocesan structure and
the diocese of Plymouth in 1850. The patron St Boniface
was born in nearby Crediton. St Mary was chosen in
reference to the initial pro-cathedral, the parish church
of St Mary on Saint Mary Street.

The newly formed diocese of Plymouth covered Dorset,
Devon and Cornwall. Whilst there was a greater number
of Catholics in Plymouth than nearby Exeter, which had
been the pre-Reformation focal point for Catholics in the
South West, this was not the only reason that Plymouth
was chosen as the Bishop's seat. More importantly, the
Roman Catholic Relief Act of 1829 made it illegal for a
new Catholic diocese to use the same name as an
existing Church of England diocese, such as Exeter.

Interestingly, the same was not true for any newly created Church of England diocese, which is why we see a number of similarly named Catholic and Church of England diocese today, such as Portsmouth.

The Cathedral Church of St Mary and St Boniface was built on the outskirts of Plymouth on Eldad Hill. As a result, a number of other Catholic churches were built in central Plymouth in the 18th and 19th centuries to be accessible for the growing Catholic community. This included both permanent residents and sailors docked in the bustling port town (or city as Plymouth became in 1928). One such church was the cathedral's chapel-of-ease on Armada Way, Christ the King Church, which was designed in the Gothic style by Sir Giles Gilbert Scott and opened in September 1962.

Plymouth Cathedral

Portsmouth Cathedral

COE – DIOCESE OF PORTSMOUTH

Cathedral Church of St Thomas,
High Street, Old Portsmouth, PO1 2HH
023 9282 3300 | www.portsmouthcathedral.org.uk

Around 1180, the wealthy Norman merchant Jean de Gissor gifted land at *Sudewede*, 'the island of Portsea', to Augustinian canons to build a chapel 'to the Glorious Honour of the Martyr Thomas of Canterbury'. Despite the cathedral's close proximity to the English Channel it managed to survive the French raids of the 14th-century Hundred Years War which decimated much of Portsmouth, and the chancel and transepts of this original Norman building survive today.

Unfortunately, the murder of the Bishop of Chichester by local seamen in 1449 meant the church was excommunicated until the 16th century. A Royalist stronghold, the church suffered substantial damage during the English Civil War but was renovated in the Classic style during the Restoration.

When the Diocese of Portsmouth was established in 1927, the church became pro-cathedral for the diocese with plans to extend it to an appropriate size as befitting a cathedral. Church architect Sir Charles Nicholson was commissioned to create the extension in the 'neo-Byzantine' style. Much of the extension work had been completed by 1939, however this was put on hold in 1940 as the Second World War progressed. A wall that was installed 'temporarily' to make the building suitable for use without the remaining extension remained in place for another fifty years. A less elaborate version of the final extension was completed from 1990–1.

There are two cathedral churches in the city. The older Roman Catholic Cathedral of St John the Evangelist is located just over a mile away next to Victoria Park and opened in 1882.

Portsmouth Cathedral

Portsmouth Cathedral

RC – DIOCESE OF PORTSMOUTH

Cathedral Church of St John the Evangelist,
Bishop Crispian Way, Portsmouth, Hampshire, PO1 3HG
0239 282 6170 | www.portsmouthCatholiccathedral.org.uk

St John's Cathedral opened for worship in August 1882
and was immediately made the Mother Church of the
new Catholic Diocese of Portsmouth.

Following the Second Catholic Relief Act of 1791, a number
of local Catholics requested that the Vicar Apostolic of the
London District (which covered Portsmouth at the time)
provide a parish priest for the area. In response to their
plea, Rev. John Cahill was appointed and he established a
chapel within a private dwelling in the town. His successor,
Rev. Joseph Knapp, established a purpose-built chapel
in Prince George Street in the Portsea area in 1796.
However, by 1877 the chapel had become too small for
the burgeoning congregation of local Catholics and
soldiers stationed in the garrison town.

Rev. John Horan, the priest at this time, purchased a new
site for a larger church on what is now known as Bishop
Crispian Way. Funding was raised via donations from the
community and a large contribution from the Duke of

Norfolk, Henry Fitzalan-Howard. Building work took place from 1879 to 1882 and was influenced by the Gothic Revival architectural style of the 19th century and architect Augustus Welby Northmore Pugin in particular. The completion of the church came as Pope Leo XIII decided to create a new diocese spanning Hampshire, Berkshire, the Isle of Wight and the Channel Islands. The Pope chose St John's Church as the cathedral for this new diocese; the Diocese of Portsmouth. From 1882–1906 further work took place on the nave, crossing, chancel and narthex to establish the cathedral as a suitable Bishop's seat. Bomb damage during the 'Blitz' of 1941 was rectified during extensive renovations from 1946–50.

Portsmouth Cathedral

Ripon Cathedral

**COE – DIOCESE OF LEEDS
(FORMERLY THE DIOCESE OF RIPON 1836–2014 AND
RIPON AND LEEDS 1999–2014)**

Cathedral Church of St Peter and St Wilfrid,
Minster Road, Ripon, HG4 1QT
01765 603462 | www.riponcathedral.org.uk

The site of the current Ripon Cathedral initially housed
a monastery established by Scottish monks in the 660s.
Saint Spell Wilfrid, abbot of Ripon Monastery, built
one of England's first stone churches there in AD 672.
The church and accompanying crypt were built in the
style of the basilicas he had experienced in Rome.
The crypt is still intact today beneath the impressive
12th-century minster built by Archbishop of York,
Roger de Pont l'Evêques.

Spell Wilfrid dedicated the initial church to St Peter as
a symbol of his commitment to Christianity when
Northumbria still favoured Celtic traditions. Wilfred
founded other churches and monasteries but Ripon was
said to be his favourite and his final resting place after
his death in AD 710. Whilst the original church was
destroyed by Vikings, it has since been rebuilt to varying
degrees and the current cathedral is the fourth church

building to have occupied the site. Roger de Pont l'Evêque rebuilt the church as Ripon Minster, the mother church for the then Diocese of York, in an impressive Early English Gothic style. The crypt was incorporated to encourage pilgrims to visit St Wilfrid's tomb.

In 1836 the church became the cathedral for the Diocese of Ripon, the first Anglican diocese to be created since the Reformation. In 2014, the more recent Diocese of Ripon and Leeds was included within the new Diocese of Leeds. Uniquely for the Church of England, the Diocese of Leeds has three cathedrals in one diocese; Bradford, Ripon and Wakefield. It is run by the Bishop of Leeds alongside area bishops (Deans) at each cathedral.

Ripon Cathedral

Rochester Cathedral

COE – DIOCESE OF ROCHESTER

The Cathedral Church of Christ and the
Blessed Virgin Mary,
Garth House, The Precinct, Rochester, Kent, ME1 1SX
01634 843366 | www.rochestercathedral.org

Similarly to many of Britain's cathedrals, Rochester was
built on the site of an earlier Anglo-Saxon church dating
from around AD 604. However, by the time of the
Norman Conquest this structure was in a state of disrepair
and by 1083 building work had commenced on a new
cathedral. Consecrated in 1130, with King Henry I in
attendance, the cathedral survived at least three fires in
its first fifty years of service.

In the 13th century the cathedral became a place of
pilgrimage following the death of Saint William of Perth.
William was a Scottish baker who was murdered close to
the cathedral in 1201. Soon after William's death, tales
of miracles were reported close to his shrine leading to
him being acclaimed a saint by local people. In 1215
the cathedral was looted by the forces of King John I,
and desecrated by the troops of Simon de Montfort,
6th Earl of Leicester, in 1264. Numerous alterations
and additions were made to the cathedral over the next

four centuries, but by the time of the Restoration the building's fabric was in a poor state of repair. The following centuries have seen almost continuous repair and restoration work.

Rochester Cathedral

St Albans Cathedral

COE – DIOCESE OF ST ALBANS

The Cathedral and Abbey Church of St Alban,
Sumpter Yard, St Albans, Hertfordshire, AL1 1BY
01727 890210 | www.stalbanscathedral.org

Saint Alban is said to be the first-recorded British Christian
martyr, beheaded at the Roman Britain town of
Verulamium for his Christian faith. St Alban's Cathedral
was built close to the site of Saint Alban's execution in
the 3rd or 4th century AD. The first abbey was
commissioned by the Anglo-Saxon king Offa of Mercia
(famous for building Offa's Dyke).

Following the Norman Conquest a new abbey was built
using some of the stones and bricks from Verulamium.
Completed in 1115, the building suffered earthquake
damage in 1250 and went into a period of slow decline
following the Dissolution of the Monasteries and its
conversion from an abbey to a parish church. It was not
until the 19th century that sufficient funds were allocated
to undertake any meaningful repairs, and in 1877 the old
abbey church became the cathedral for the new diocese
of St Albans. Today, due to the unusual history of the
cathedral, it bears a duality of purpose as both a parish
church and a fully-fledged cathedral.

St Edmundsbury Cathedral

COE – DIOCESE OF ST EDMUNDSBURY AND IPSWICH

Cathedral Church of St James and St Edmund,
Angel Hill, Bury St Edmunds, IP33 1LS
01284 748720 | www.stedscathedral.co.uk

Also referred to as 'Bury St Edmunds Cathedral' due to
its location, St Edmundsbury Cathedral is the seat of the
Bishop of St Edmundsbury and Ipswich. The town itself
was a royal Saxon 'borough' and a monastery has been
present on the site since around AD 633. The cathedral
and surrounding area owe the rest of their name to the
later East Angles king and future patron saint of England;
Edmund. Edmund was killed by Danish Vikings in AD 869.
His body was moved to the site around AD 900 and it
became a popular place of pilgrimage around which the
Benedictine Abbey 'St Edmundsbury' was founded by
King Canute in 1020. The name of the town that
sprung up around this new pilgrimage site changed
from Beodricsworth to St Edmundsbury accordingly.
Whilst the abbey itself fell into ruin after Henry VIII's
Dissolution of the Monasteries, the parish church
which has stood since 1056 has remained. It was rebuilt
over the next few hundred years before becoming
St Edmundsbury Cathedral in 1914 with the introduction
of the new Diocese of St Edmundsbury and Ipswich.

St Paul's Cathedral, London

COE – DIOCESE OF LONDON

St Paul's Cathedral,
St Paul's Churchyard, London, EC4M 8AD
0207 246 8350 | www.stpauls.co.uk

A cathedral dedicated to Saint Paul has stood atop Ludgate Hill, the highest point in the City of London, for more than 1,400 years. The present structure, whose iconic dome dominates the London skyline, is the masterpiece of Sir Christopher Wren. Built between 1675 and 1710, it is at least the fourth cathedral to have stood on the site and was built after its predecessor was destroyed by the Great Fire of London in 1666.

The first St Paul's Cathedral was founded in AD 604 by Saint Mellitus, a monk who had travelled to Britain with St Augustine. Despite a brief return to paganism, the city returned to the Roman Church under Saint Erkenwald, who became Bishop of London in AD 675. The initial cathedral buildings suffered both fire damage and plundering by Vikings and it was not until 1087 that a more permanent Norman structure was put in place by Bishop Maurice. The cathedral flourished for nearly 600 years, surviving the 16th-century Reformation of the Church in England and the neglect of the Civil War from 1642, only to be destroyed by The Great Fire of London in September 1666, a week after plans had been made for a major restoration. Sir Christopher Wren, who had already undertaken to complete the restoration of the previous building, spent nine years meticulously planning the new cathedral before construction began in 1675. Fittingly, the final structural stone of the new cathedral was laid by Wren's son, Christopher Wren junior, on 26 October 1708. Since the 18th century, despite structural instability and the impact of two bomb strikes during the Second World War, St Paul's remains an iconic place of worship to Christians worldwide.

St Paul's Cathedral

Salford Cathedral

RC – DIOCESE OF SALFORD

The Cathedral Church of St John the Evangelist,
250 Chapel Street, Salford, M3 5LE
0161 817 2210 | www.dioceseofsalford.org.uk/
diocese/visiting-us/cathedral

Building work on Salford Cathedral began in 1844, using
designs modelled on several existing medieval churches.
For example, the choir and sanctuary are of a similar type
to those of Selby Abbey, whereas the spire is modelled
on that of St Mary Magdalene in Newark-on-Trent.
Building work on the church took four years, and it was
opened on 9 August 1848 by Bishop George Brown.
After the restoration of the Catholic hierarchy in 1850,
the church was elevated to cathedral status in 1852,
making it one of the first of four new Catholic cathedrals
in England and Wales since the English Reformation.
A storm in 1881 caused some damage to the cathedral's
spire, but funds were soon raised for repairs and
refurbishment. By 1890 the church's debts had been paid
off, and the cathedral was consecrated. Various repairs
and minor alterations were made to the cathedral's
structure in the early and mid-20th century, including
repair to damage sustained during the Second World War.

Salisbury Cathedral

COE – DIOCESE OF SALISBURY

The Cathedral Church of the Blessed Virgin Mary,
6 The Close, Salisbury, SP1 2EJ
01722 555120 | www.salisburycathedral.org.uk

The original Salisbury Cathedral was actually located in Old Sarum, some two miles north of the modern-day city. The new cathedral, built over thirty-eight years, had its foundation stone laid in 1220 and was fully consecrated by 1258. Since 1549, Salisbury has had the tallest church spire in the country (owing to Lincoln Cathedral's spire collapsing in the same year), as well as the largest cathedral close in Britain.

In 1668 Sir Christopher Wren was drafted in to provide a report on the condition of the cathedral's fabric, during which he noticed that the spire's supporting pillars were beginning to buckle under the immense weight of the stonework. Wren suggested that the spire be strengthened with internal iron bands and his recommendation was carried out in 1670. On display in the chapter house at Salisbury is the best preserved of the four surviving original copies of Magna Carta.

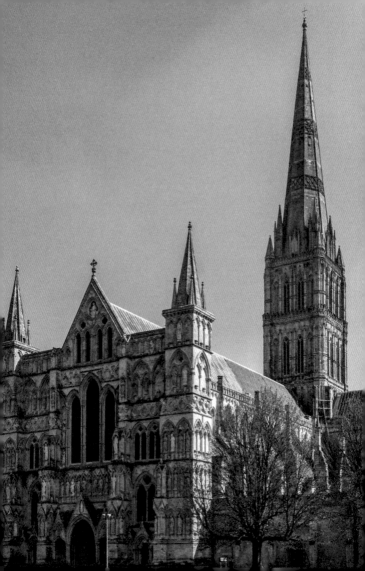

Sheffield Cathedral

COE – DIOCESE OF SHEFFIELD

The Cathedral Church of St Peter and St Paul,
Church Street, Sheffield, S1 1HA
0114 275 3434 | www.sheffieldcathedral.org

Built on a much earlier Anglo-Saxon religious site,
Sheffield Cathedral is the oldest building in Sheffield still
in daily use. The building has been subject to numerous
alterations and additions over the centuries, with the
oldest part of the cathedral boasting stonework from
the late Norman era. In 1914 the church of St Peter and
St Paul (formerly dedicated to St Peter and the Holy
Trinity) was elevated to cathedral status following the
creation of the Diocese of Sheffield, although it also
remained a parish church for the smaller Parish of
Sheffield. Shortly afterwards, plans were made to enlarge
the church and to reorient it by 90 degrees but these
plans were interrupted by the onset of the Second World
War, after which they were discarded entirely. Recent
heritage lottery funding has improved access and
brought new exhibitions to the cathedral's floorspace,
and today the structure is one of only five Grade I listed
buildings in the city.

Sheffield Cathedral

RC – DIOCESE OF HALLAM

The Cathedral Church of St Marie,
Cathedral House, Norfolk Street, Sheffield, S1 2JB
0114 272 2522 | stmariecathedral.org

The fact that Sheffield Cathedral is not immediately visible gives some clue as to its heritage. Beginning life as a small chapel in the early 1800s, it was a requirement of the time for any Catholic places of worship to be set back from public roadways. Almost as soon as the chapel was built, an influx of Irish and European Catholic immigrants into Sheffield necessitated a larger building and in 1850 the present structure was completed. However, this was to be a particularly expensive building project and it was not until 1889 that the church was completely free of debt and was able to be consecrated. During the Second World War, a bomb destroyed many of the stained glass windows in the church, with the rest being removed to a place of safety until 1947. In 1980, on the creation of the Diocese of Hallam, The Church of St Marie was raised to cathedral status. In addition to being a place of worship, today the cathedral also plays host to regular choral concerts.

Shrewsbury Cathedral

RC – DIOCESE OF SHREWSBURY

The Cathedral Church of Our Lady Help of Christians
and St Peter of Alcantara,
Cathedral House, 11 Belmont, Shrewsbury, SY1 1TE
01743 290000 | www.shrewsburycathedral.org

Completed in 1856, Shrewsbury Cathedral was designed
by Edward Pugin although it was actually Edward's father,
Augustus Welby Northmore Pugin, who was intended as
architect. Unfortunately, Augustus died before work began
so the mantle was handed over to his son instead. Initial
designs for the cathedral included a tall spire but once
ground had been broken it was found that a stratum of
sand was precariously close to the building's foundations
and the spire had to be abandoned. During the interwar
period, six of the ten stained glass windows were created
by the renowned artist Margate Rope, a local parishioner
who later became a Carmelite nun. Rope also designed
the cathedral's war memorial, which stands on the west
porch, dedicated to sixty-three local men who died during
the First World War. The cathedral was re-ordered in
1984 to make it more practical for modern services and
a new altar was consecrated a year later in 1985.

Southwark Cathedral

COE – DIOCESE OF SOUTHWARK

The Cathedral and Collegiate Church of St Saviour
and St Mary Overie,
London Bridge, London, SE1 9DA
020 7367 6700 | cathedral.southwark.anglican.org

The Cathedral and Collegiate Church of St Saviour and
St Mary Overie (which translates to 'over the river') has
been a place of Christian worship since 1086, and likely
for some time before. First a collegiate church, and from
1106 an Augustinian priory, the church fell under the
patronage of the Bishops of Westminster who had their
London residence just a few yards away. The church in
its present form dates from between 1220 and 1420
after the Great Fire of 1212 destroyed much of the old
structure. During the Dissolution of the Monasteries the
church became the property of King Henry VIII in 1539
and he rededicated it to St Saviour. Later sold by King
James VI and I to wealthy members of the local
congregation, by the 19th century the church was in
need of substantial repairs and was at risk of being
demolished. Luckily the decision was made to restore
the building and in 1905 when the diocese of Southwark
was created the church was raised to cathedral status.

Southwark, St George's Cathedral

RC — ARCHDIOCESE OF SOUTHWARK

The Metropolitan Cathedral Church of St George,
Cathedral House, Westminster Bridge Road,
London, SE1 7HY
020 7928 5256 | www.stgeorgescathedral.org.uk

Situated opposite the Imperial War Museum, St George's
is the seat of the Archbishop of Southwark plus the mother
church for the archdiocese of Southwark and the dioceses
of Arundel and Brighton, Portsmouth, and Plymouth.
The cathedral was built in 1848 to accommodate a large
influx of recent Irish immigrants into the area and in
1852 it became one of the first Catholic churches to be
raised to cathedral status since the English Reformation.
Designed by renowned architect Augustus Welby
Northmore Pugin, who also worked on the Houses of
Parliament, the structure was badly damaged during
Second World War bombing raids and was only reopened
in 1958. Pope John Paul II visited the cathedral in 1982,
with his visit having since been commemorated in
stained glass.

Southwell Minster

COE – DIOCESE OF SOUTHWELL AND NOTTINGHAM

Cathedral and Parish Church of the
Blessed Virgin Mary,
Church Street, Southwell, Nottinghamshire, NG25 0HD
01636 812649 | www.southwellminster.org

Built on the site of an earlier Anglo-Saxon church
(and prior to that a Roman villa), construction on
Southwell Minster began in 1108 and was completed
by around 1150. The twin pepperpot towers on the west
front were completed by 1170. Located next to the
Archbishop of York's palace, which doubled as a centre
for theological study, the church was designated as a
minster and it continues to carry the name today.
Some additions were carried out in the 13th and early
14th centuries, including the building of the minster's
Chapter House. Unfortunately, the building was
seriously damaged during the English Civil War and
extensive repairs were needed in the following decades.
By the early 19th century the minster's structure was in
poor condition and in 1815 the iconic twin pepperpot
spires were deemed unsafe and subsequently removed.
They were not replaced until the early 1880s, when the
minster also became a fully fledged cathedral with the

creation of the new Diocese of Southwell. Today, a few elements of the old Anglo-Saxon structure can still be seen, including some flooring and tympanum in the north transept. At the west end of the Nave is the Angel Window. Installed in 1996, this large perpendicular window was designed and painted by Patrick Reyntiens.

Southwell Minster

Truro Cathedral

COE – DIOCESE OF TRURO

Cathedral of the Blessed Virgin Mary,
14 St Mary's Street, Truro, TR1 2AF
01872 276782 | www.trurocathedral.org.uk

One of the newer Church of England cathedrals,
construction on Truro Cathedral began shortly after the
creation of the Diocese of Truro in 1876. Situated on the
site of a previous church (St Mary's), the service of
consecration took place in 1887 although the cathedral
building wasn't fully completed until 1910. The cathedral
was built in a Gothic Revival design by the renowned
architect John Loughborough Pearson. It is also one of
only three churches in the United Kingdom to have three
spires (the others being Lichfield Cathedral and the
Scottish St Mary's Episcopal Cathedral in Edinburgh;
unfortunately Lincoln Cathedral lost its third spire in 1549
and it was never rebuilt). Even though it is a relatively
new cathedral, restoration work has been ongoing since
2002, with stonework erosion being of particular concern.

Wakefield Cathedral

COE – DIOCESE OF LEEDS

Cathedral Church of All Saints,
Northgate, Wakefield, WF1 1HG
01924 373923 | www.wakefieldcathedral.org.uk

The Cathedral Church of All Saints is situated in the centre
of Wakefield on the site of an ancient Saxon church.
In 1090, William II gifted the church's land to Lewes
Priory and a new church was built. The church was then
rebuilt in 1329 and reconstructed again in 1469. By the
Victorian era the church was in a state of serious neglect
and thus began a protracted period of restoration
undertaken by Sir George Gilbert Scott. In 1888, All Saints
Church (as it was known then) was raised to cathedral
status when the Diocese of Wakefield was created. Today
it serves as both a parish church and a cathedral.
Historical highlights include medieval choir stalls and
15th-century timber ceilings. The oldest part of the
church is the wall of the north aisle, which dates from
around 1150.

Wells Cathedral

COE – DIOCESE OF BATH AND WELLS

The Cathedral Church of St Andrew,
Cathedral Green, Wells, Somerset, BA5 2UE
01749 674483 | www.wellscathedral.org.uk

The first church was established on the site in AD 705 by
Aldhelm, abbot of nearby Malmesbury Abbey. Construction
of the present cathedral began in 1175 and was largely
complete at the time of its dedication in 1239. Many
historians consider Wells to be the first truly Gothic
cathedral in Europe and around 300 of its original medieval
statues can still be seen on the exterior of the building.
Various additions and alterations were made to the
cathedral through the rest of the medieval period, and
– apart from fifteen years of closure during the
Commonwealth Parliament – the cathedral has been
relatively unaffected by religious turmoil throughout
the centuries.

The cathedral has several significant features. This includes
the Jesse Window, which contains stained glass dating
from and the 14th century, the scissor arches, built by
master mason William Joy between 1338–48 to
strengthen the cathedral and prevent collapse of the
tower. The Wells Clock is considered the second-oldest

clock mechanism in Britain to survive in original condition and still be in use. Also the nearby Vicars' Close is thought to be the oldest residential street in Europe, built to house the Vicars Choral, who were the men of the cathedral choir. The street dates from the 14th century.

Wells Cathedral

Westminster Cathedral

Metropolitan Cathedral of the Precious Blood
of Our Lord Jesus Christ,
42 Francis Street, Westminster, London, SW1P 1QW
020 7798 9055 | www.westminstercathedral.org.uk

Westminster Cathedral is the mother church of Roman
Catholicism in England (and Wales) and it is also the
largest Catholic church building in the country. Before
the land was purchased by the Catholic Church in 1884,
the site had been home to a prison, a bull-baiting ring, a
maze and a pleasure garden. Work began on the present
structure in 1895 following the Catholic emancipation of
the preceding 150 years. Architect John Francis Bentley
used a design heavily influenced by Byzantine architecture.
Opened in 1903, just one year after Bentley's death, much
of the interior was (and still is) unfinished owing to financial
reasons. As a consequence, its consecration was delayed
until 1910. In more recent years both Pope John Paul II
and Pope Benedict XVI have celebrated Mass in the
cathedral and in 1995 Queen Elizabeth II attended
Choral Vespers here.

Winchester Cathedral

COE – DIOCESE OF WINCHESTER

Cathedral Church of the Holy Trinity, and of St Peter
and St Paul and of St Swithun,
9 The Close, Winchester, SO23 9LS
01962 857200 | www.winchester-cathedral.org.uk

The original cathedral was founded close to the site of
the current building in AD 648, when Wessex's pagan
monarchy first converted to Christianity. Known as the
Old Minster, it was demolished in 1093 immediately
after the consecration of its new Norman successor.
Much of this 'new' cathedral survives today, including
the crypt, transepts and parts of the nave. Many more
alterations were carried out to the structure over the
medieval period and by the early 16th century much of
the cathedral resembled the structure we see today.
Surveys in the early 1900s showed that the east end of
the structure was at risk of collapsing due to centuries of
subsidence, and it was only thanks to a deep-sea diver
called William Walker that the cathedral is still standing
today. He spent six years working in total darkness
shoring up the foundations with concrete and bricks!
As well as being the final resting place for numerous
kings and queens throughout history, Winchester
Cathedral is also where Jane Austen was interred.

Worcester Cathedral

COE – DIOCESE OF WORCESTER

The Cathedral Church of Christ and the Blessed Mary
the Virgin of Worcester,
8 College Yard, Worcester, WR1 2LA
01905 732900 | www.worcestercathedral.co.uk

Worcester Cathedral, along with its Diocese, was
founded in AD 680 and Bishop Bosel was consecrated
as the cathedral's first bishop. Some 300 years later in
AD 983, Saint Oswald built a new cathedral dedicated to
St Mary and an accompanying Benedictine monastery.
A centre for learning throughout the Middle Ages,
Worcester's Benedictine monks studied all manner of
subjects at university such as theology, medicine, law,
history, mathematics, physics and astronomy. A number
of their medieval textbooks can still be found in the
cathedral's library.

Following the Norman Conquest, the cathedral was
rebuilt once more by Bishop Wulfstan in 1084 and parts
of this structure are still visible today. The Benedictine
monastery adjoining the cathedral flourished until it was
dissolved in 1540 by Henry VIII's English Reformation,
although small sections of the monastic remains can still
be seen in the cathedral's grounds. The cathedral was

badly damaged in the English Civil War, but was soon repaired after the restoration of the monarchy. In 1860, the cathedral underwent another period of major restoration with much of the current external stonework dating from this period. Worcester Cathedral is also the resting place of King John I. He was interred in front of the altar of St Wulfstan before being moved into a more elaborate sarcophagus and accompanying effigy in 1232.

Worcester Cathedral

York Minster

COE — DIOCESE OF YORK

The Cathedral and Metropolitical Church of
St Peter in York,
Deangate, York, YO1 7HH
01904 557200 | yorkminster.org

York Minster is the seat of the Archbishop of York, the second-highest office of the Church of England after the Archbishop of Canterbury. The first recorded church on the site was a hastily constructed wooden structure, allowing a recently converted Edwin, King of Northumbria, to be baptised. By AD 637, a stone structure had been built on the site in dedication to Saint Peter although by AD 670 it had fallen into disrepair. Despite being repaired in successive decades with the addition of a school and library the church was destroyed by a fire in AD 741 and had to be rebuilt once again. After the Norman Conquest the new Archbishop of York, Thomas of Bayeux, rebuilt York Minster. The foundations of this 11th-century building can still be seen today.

The present building dates from the 1230s but has seen numerous additions and alterations in its 800-year history. A survey in 1967 showed that the building was close to collapse, and during subsequent renovation work the remains of a Roman fort were found under the south transept. Interestingly, the Minster is one of only seven cathedrals in the world to have its own police force.

English Cathedrals which are home to other Christian denominations

Most of the Cathedrals still in use for Christian worship in England today are home to the Church of England and Roman Catholic faiths. However, there are also a number of religious buildings which have been consecrated as Cathedrals and are home to other Christian denominations. More information on these Cathedrals can be found below.

Catholic denominations

The Cathedral Church of the Holy Family in Exile (Ukrainian Catholic Church)
Duke Street, London, W1K 5BQ
020 7629 1534 | parish.rcdow.org.uk/ukrainianchurch

The Cathedral Church of the Holy Family in Exile was consecrated in 1968 and is considered part of the Catholic Diocese of Westminster in terms of location. However, jurisdictionally it is overseen by the Ukrainian Catholic Eparchial bishop.

Pro-Cathedral Church of St Augustine, Canterbury, Kent
(Anglican Catholic Church)
Eastling Road, Painters Forstal, Nr Faversham, Kent, ME13 0DU
01797 321704 | www.anglicancatholic.org.uk/church-of-st-augustine-of-canterbury

The Anglican Catholic Church was first established in the late 1970s in response to increasing liberalisation of member churches within the Anglican Communion. The Diocese of the United Kingdom was formally established in 1992. St Augustine's Church was established as a place of worship in May 2005 and became Pro-Cathedral in 2008 when the Church's Priest Ordinary was consecrated as the Bishop Ordinary of the Diocese of the United Kingdom.

All Saints Liberal Catholic Pro-Cathedral Church (Liberal Catholic Church)
205c Upper Richmond Road, Putney, London, SW15 6SQ
all-saints-lcc.weebly.com

Also referred to as Putney Cathedral, All Saints Pro-Cathedral is home to the Liberal Catholic Church. The Liberal Catholic Church has links to the ancient Catholic See of Utrecht in the Netherlands, from which the European 'Old Catholic Church' was formed in 1870. The Liberal Catholic Church was introduced in Great Britain in the early 20th century following a period of reform in the Old Catholic Church. James Ingall Wegwood became the first Presiding Bishop in 1916. The Liberal Catholic Church is an independent and autonomous body, independent of Rome and responsible for its own administration.

Eastern and Oriental Orthodox Churches

The term 'Orthodox' in a religious sense refers to the 'right opinion' and conforming to accepted beliefs. Similarly to the Catholic and Protestant religions, the Orthodox Church believes in the role of Jesus Christ, his crucifixion and resurrection. There were strong links between the Eastern Orthodox Church, the Oriental Orthodox Church and the Roman Catholic Church until AD 451 when the Oriental Orthodoxy split to follow the See of Alexandria in Egypt. In AD 1054 the Eastern Orthodox Church split from the Roman Catholic Church and the authority of the Pope in Rome to follow the See of Constantinople. Both the Eastern and Oriental Orthodox Churches include autocephalous churches (or Cathedrals) which means their Bishops have a greater level of autonomy.

Houses of worship for members of the Antiochian, Coptic, Greek, Russian, Syriac and Ukrainian Autocephalous Orthodox Church have been established in England and include the following Cathedrals.

Cathedral Church of St George (Antiochian Orthodox Church)
1A Redhill Street, London, NW1 4BG
0207 383 0403 | www.antiochianorth.co.uk

The Cathedral was originally built in 1837 as the Anglican Christ Church and the funeral service for the prominent writer George Orwell was held here in 1950. The Cathedral Church of St George was established as an Antiochian Orthodox Cathedral in 1989, one of only two Antiochian places of worship in London.

St. George's Cathedral, Stevenage (Coptic Orthodox Church)
Broadhall Way, Stevenage, SG2 8NP
020 7993 9001 | www.copticcentre.com/st-georges-cathedral

The first Coptic Orthodox service to be held in England took place in August 1954 at a meeting of the World Council of Churches. From 1969, regular services were held throughout the United Kingdom and the Parish of St George's was established in 1991. The Coptic Orthodox Cathedral of Saint George, the first purpose-built Coptic Orthodox place of worship in the United Kingdom, was built in 2000.

The Greek Orthodox Cathedral of the Dormition of the Mother of God and St Andrew (Greek Orthodox Church)
8 Arthur Place, Summerhill, B1 3DA
0121 236 3274 | www.orthandrew.co.uk

A Greek Orthodox Community was established in Birmingham in the aftermath of the Second World War. Residents would travel to churches in London and Manchester until 1947 when visiting priests were sent to deliver a monthly liturgy service by the Archbishop of Thyateira. The current Cathedral was a former Church of England church which served as a Greek Orthodox parish church from 1958 until it was consecrated as a Cathedral in 1980.

The Greek Orthodox Church of Saint Nicholas and Saint Xenophon (Greek Orthodox Church)
Aylestone Road, Leicester, LE2 7NW
0116 291 6518 | greekchurchleicester.com

The Greek Orthodox community of St Nicholas and St Xenophon of Leicester was established in the 1960s. The current Cathedral, formerly All Souls Church of England parish church, was established in 1986.

Greek Orthodox Cathedral Church of All Saints (Greek Orthodox Church)
Camden Street, London, NW1 0JA
020 7485 2149 | www.gocas.org

The Cathedral was originally built as an Anglican Church known as the Camden Chapel in 1824. It was renamed twice, first to St Stephen's Church and later to All Saints Church. The dedication to All Saints was retained by the Greek Orthodox community who took over the building in 1948.

The Greek Orthodox Cathedral of the Holy Wisdom of God, also known as St Sophia's Cathedral (Greek Orthodox Church)
Moscow Road, Bayswater, London, W2 4LQ
020 7229 7260 | www.stsophia.org.uk

The first Greek Orthodox Church to be established in London was the Cathedral Church of the Dormition of the Mother of God. It was built in 1677 in Soho and funded by the local Greek Orthodox Community before being disbanded in 1684. The Cathedral of the Holy Wisdom of God was later built in 1877 to accommodate the Greek Orthodox Community in nearby Lancaster Gate and Bayswater.

Cathedral Church of the Nativity of the Mother of God, also known as St Mary's Cathedral (Greek Orthodox Church)
305 Camberwell New Road, London, SE5 0TF
020 7703 0137 | stmarysgreekorthodox.wixsite.com/camberwell

The Cathedral was originally built as a Catholic Apostolic Church in 1876. In 1963 it was given to the Greek Orthodox Community who later bought the building in 1977 and established a Greek school.

The Greek Orthodox Cathedral of St Andrew (Greek Orthodox Church)
Kentish Town Road, London, NW1 9QA
020 7485 6385/0198 | www.standrewsgreekorthodoxcathedral.co.uk

Originally built as the Anglican parish church of St Barnabas in 1884, the building has been used by the Greek Orthodox Church since 1957 and was established as a Greek Orthodox Cathedral in 1970.

The Greek Orthodox Cathedral of the Holy Cross and St Michael (Greek Orthodox)
Golders Green Road, London, NW11 8HL
0208 455 75 10 | hwww.archangel.me.uk

Originally built as the Church of England parish church of St Michael's in 1914, the Greek Orthodox Community began to share use of the church in 1970. The building was deconsecrated as a Church of England church in 1979 and taken over by a varied Eastern and Oriental Orthodox congregation.

Cathedral of the Dormition and All Saints (Russian Orthodox Church)
67 Ennismore Gardens, London, SW7 1NH
0207 584 0096 | www.sourozh.org/directions-old

Originally built in 1849 as the Anglican Church of All Saints. The All Saints parish merged with another Anglican church nearby in 1955 and the building was no longer needed. It was given to the Russian Orthodox Church and consecrated in 1956. In 1978 the building was bought by the Russian Sourozh Diocese.

Cathedral of the Dormition of the Most Holy Mother of God and
Holy Royal Martyrs (Russian Orthodox Church)
57 Harvard Road, London, W4 4ED
0203 6426 459 | www.russianchurchlondon.org/en

Located in Chiswick, services at the Cathedral are held in Church Slavonic (liturgical language of the Russian Orthodox Church) with some English translations.

St Thomas' Cathedral, East Acton, Cathedral Church of Saint Thomas
(Syriac (Syrian) Orthodox Church)
7–11 Armstrong Road, London, W3 7JL
www.syrianorthodoxchurch.net

The Syriac Orthodox Church was established in the United Kingdom in the 1960s. Visiting priests and bishops supported the community and services were held in various houses of worship until a permanent priest (later promoted to Bishop) was appointed in 1994. St Thomas' Cathedral was consecrated in 2010 as a permanent home for the Syriac Orthodox Church community.

Cathedral of the Holy Transfiguration of our Saviour
(Ukrainian Autocephalous Orthodox Church of Great Britain)
1a Newton Ave, London, W3 8AJ
020 8992 4689 | uaoc-london.org

In the aftermath of the Second World War Ukrainian communities were established across the country and formed the wider community of the Ukrainian Autocephalous Orthodox Church in Great Britain. With the support of the community an existing church was purchased in London in 1977 and this became the Ukrainian Autocephalous Orthodox Cathedral.

Image credits

Collins

LITTLE BOOKS

These beautifully presented Little Books make excellent pocket-sized guides, packed with hints and tips.

101 Ways to Win at Scrabble	978-0-00-758914-2	£6.99
Bananagrams® Secrets	978-0-00-825046-1	£6.99
Bridge Secrets	978-0-00-825047-8	£6.99
Card Games	978-0-00-830653-3	£6.99
Clans and Tartans	978-0-00-825109-3	£6.99
Craft Beer	978-0-00-827120-6	£6.99
English Castles	978-0-00-829833-3	£6.99
English Cathedrals	978-0-00-829832-6	£6.99
English History	978-0-00-829813-5	£6.99
Gin	978-0-00-825810-8	£6.99
Rum	978-0-00-827122-0	£6.99
Scots Dictionary	978-0-00-828552-4	£6.99
Scottish Castles	978-0-00-825111-6	£6.99
Scottish Dance	978-0-00-821056-4	£6.99
Scottish History	978-0-00-825110-9	£6.99
Scrabble Secrets	978-0-00-829022-1	£6.99
Whisky	978-0-00-825108-6	£6.99

Available to buy from all good booksellers and online.
All titles are also available as ebooks.
www.collins.co.uk

 @collins_ref facebook.com/collinsref